# Every Cat Has A Story

*True Stories Exploring
the Spiritual Connection of Felines
with Their Beloved Owners*

Compiled and written by
## Jasmine Kinnear

**CCB Publishing
British Columbia, Canada**

Every Cat Has A Story: True Stories Exploring the Spiritual
Connection of Felines with Their Beloved Owners

Copyright © 2007 compiled and written by Jasmine Kinnear
ISBN-13: 978-0-9783893-8-3
First Edition


Library and Archives Canada Cataloguing in Publication
Kinnear, Jasmine, 1953-
Every Cat Has A Story: True stories exploring the spiritual connection of
felines with their beloved owners / compiled and written by Jasmine
Kinnear.
Also available in electronic format.
ISBN 978-0-9783893-8-3
1. Cats--Anecdotes. 2. Cats--Religious aspects. 3. Human-animal
relationships. I. Title.
SF445.5.K55 2007   636.8'0887   C2007-906059-5

Publisher:    CCB Publishing
              British Columbia, Canada
              www.ccbpublishing.com

For my beloved father,
Donald Thomas Hutchinson.
Daddy, you were the only light in my childhood.

With my love,
xoxo dj

*Artists like cats; soldiers like dogs.*
**- Desmond Morris**

## *Other books by Jasmine Kinnear*

Proven Marketing Tips for the Successful Cat Breeder

How to Hide Your Cat From the Landlord

## *Jasmine Kinnear's upcoming books:*

Insider's Guide to Buying Purebred Kittens

Insider's Guide to Starting & Managing a Cattery

More books in the *Every Story* series are also forthcoming.
See page 6 for additional details.

# Contributing Authors

We would like to acknowledge individual authors for permission to reprint the following material contained in this book. Please note that the stories written solely by Jasmine Kinnear are not included in this listing.

1) Nick L. Sacco, Raytown, Missouri, USA
   *The Blue Angel & Her Garden of Pets*
2) Robin Doll, USA
   *My Cat Is So Insolent, She Has A Price on Her Head*
3) Esther Sustersich, Courtney, British Columbia, Canada
   *The Ugliest Cat*
4) Pat Chalmers, Corby, Northamptonshire, UK
   *Barney, The Green Pawed Moggie*
5) Sande Kay, California, USA
   *True Reflections*

# *Do You Have a Story to Share?*

Do you or someone you know have a heart warming, touching or loving story, poem or article about a cat, dog, mother, daughter, teacher, nurse, etc.? Why not share it with the rest of the world? We welcome stories from those not given a chance to honour an experience that left a lasting impression and significantly touched their lives. If you feel it belongs in a future volume of this series please send it to us:

CCB Publishing
e-mail: submissions@ccbpublishing.com

We will make sure that you and/or the author are credited for the contribution. Thank you.

A sampling of future volumes in the *Every Story* series includes:

*Every Cat Has A Story (Volume 2)*
*Every Dog Has A Story*
*Every Mother Has A Story*
*Every Daughter Has A Story*
*Every Sister Has A Story*
*Every Father Has A Story*
*Every Grandparent Has A Story*
*Every Single Mother Has A Story*
*Every Working Woman Has A Story*
*Every Teacher Has A Story*
*Every Nurse Has A Story*

and many more... for additional information visit:
www.ccbpublishing.com

# Preface

We each have our own perception of the most beautiful species that grace God's earth. From my perspective even as a child, the most elegant of all his creations has remained the cat. My fascination with them began in early childhood and has developed into a lifetime love affair; I see an exquisite beauty in all felines whether born moggie and domestic or purebred with an impressive pedigree.

After living with countless felines during my breeding career there is a distinct possibility that I may have taken my passion to an extreme. Such devotion has, for example, blessed me with an ability to connect to the source creating a feline's anxiety within their home. My purpose is to serve as a verbal bridge of understanding between an owner and their beloved cat when problems occur. I literally serve as the cat's voice, informing the owner of the unknown source creating the behavioural problem. Success is often determined when the owner is willing to implement the changes I have suggested as their feline will respond in kind. When an owner has become desperate for a solution to a long-term problem, the changes in the feline's behaviour have literally saved the cat's life.

A dear friend and colleague confided that possibly my success has been due to my unique approach with felines. She was often with me during feline consultations and has provided valuable feedback after reading my books. She believes that after 25 years of cohabitating with hundreds of cats I have apparently developed an ability of thinking just like a cat.

I'm not sure exactly when my passion for felines began as my father never permitted a kitten in our home. In denying himself the pleasure of loving a cat he didn't realize until much later in his life exactly how much he'd missed. However as a child I was forced to accept that our home would never be blessed with a cat as his sole preference remained a devotion for dogs. He thought cats to be sneaky and untrustworthy; yet before his death he also grew to appreciate their beauty.

*Some people say that cats are sneaky, evil, and cruel.*
*True, and they have many other fine qualities as well.*
**- Missy Dizick**

On the special Christmas when I announced my first and only pregnancy he finally came to my apartment for turkey dinner. My father was a paraplegic and travelling was painfully difficult for him, however this was now a special occasion. He'd heard me speak of my two precious males for many years and upon first meeting, he surprised me by warmly bonding with them.

Dustin, my very first cat, had been rescued when five weeks old from within the fields of a local prison by an inmate. Thomas, a sweet tabby male, I'd personally rescued six months later during a snowstorm. The boys bonded and were well matched with Thomas becoming Dustin's devoted companion.

Thomas had been given my father's middle name and never left my Dad's lap the entire evening. Whether it was Thomas' affectionate nature or possibly being his namesake my Dad appeared quite pleased by his attention. My father made a comment at the time that he'd doubted anyone else would ever carry his name. Although my father was seldom wrong, in this particular instance I had been saving a surprise for him. He lived just long enough to be told the name of his newly born grandson. Although fate may have prevented him enough time to hold my baby, it is with great pride that my son bears the name of Mark Donald.

How profound then that I feel compelled to dedicate this book of feline love stories to my father's memory. I believe that such an awareness would provide him with the greatest pleasure and he would be quite pleased. Only recently has my mother mentioned that when I was a child she would often discover small saucers left under my bed for my latest feline guest. She would silently remove them and say nothing to my Dad, somehow sensing the importance of my feline connections. My darling father was never aware of the many pregnant queens that I snuck through my bedroom window as a young child. During the raging winter storms in Greenfield Park, Quebec, my bedroom became a pregnant queen's haven; the dye was cast, my cat breeding career had begun.

Jasmine, age 2

*A cat stretches from one end*
*of my childhood to the other.*
**- Blaga Dimitrova**

# Every Cat Has A Story

# Contents

EVERY CAT HAS A STORY

# Introduction

*Cats love one so much – more than they will allow.*
*But they have so much wisdom they keep it to themselves.*
- Mary Wilkins

I've been an avid collector of true cat stories for many years. The first story ever told to me, *The Cat in the Woods*, appeared as a priceless gift in my early 20's. It came through a surprising source with the memory of a colleague's experiences remaining with me but left unwritten for many years. It now seems appropriate to present this vivid recollection in the first volume of *Every Cat Has A Story*.

I have felt like a feline magnet throughout my life as I've been told the most amazing and awe inspiring stories. These gems were often provided by people I had the pleasure of meeting in a curious matter of chance. Such was the case with Esther Sustersich as we stood in a long queue of book lovers one cold March morning. Her devotion for her beautiful Bowie had already compelled her to write his story. I requested if she would consider submitting her work for this book and she most graciously provided her story of Universal destiny and an unconditional love of cats.

It is also with great appreciation that I have included submissions from readers who provided their personal stories through my web site or directly to my publisher. I have felt compelled to share these true stories because as all cat people instinctively know, there is much to learn when one cat lover shares their heart with another. For me there is no greater truth than Blaga Dimitrova's quote, "A cat stretches from one end of my childhood to the other."

There are some people lost in the enchanting world of

felines however through personal endeavour they eventually find direction, as did Emma in *The Mysterious Miss Kitty*. I feel blessed to have either served a role in these stories or to have had them most graciously shared with me. From trips to the gym to cashiers in grocery stores, cat questions were asked or stories provided. No doubt a favourite pair of cat earrings or the cat t-shirt I'd worn to the gym may have prompted other cat lovers to partake in feline conversations. However in other circumstances there was little evidence to suggest that I was a cat lover until the conversation began.

> *There is, incidentally, no way of talking about cats*
> *that enables one to come off as a sane person.*
> **- Dan Greenberg**

I take pleasure in listening to many endearing feline stories shared with great enthusiasm by their owners. I watch people actually glow as they provide intimate details of their beloved cat's idiosyncrasies. As I've been told such interesting stories over the years, I've come to appreciate the synchronicity which compels them to enter my life. I've confided to my husband that when a story touches my heart, as did *The Cat in the Woods,* then I hold on to the memory for all time.

I hope to use the other stories gathered over the years in the second volume of *Every Cat Has A Story*. It was not from a lack of interest or importance, but rather due to space restrictions which my publisher deemed necessary for this volume. Therefore this is just the beginning. The first 16 stories within this volume vary from my personal experiences to those submitted by writers in Canada, the United States and the United Kingdom.

I have been delighted with the quality of stories submitted by other writers. Reading Nick L. Sacco's story about the Blue Angel, I'm left with a lump in my throat and a desire to know more about this gentleman. I sense his life's travels have provided him with a compassion not always accessible in every man. I would enjoy reading more of his experiences and other stories that have inspired him in his journey through life.

Recently pet owners were dealt a severe emotional blow of possibly purchasing and feeding tainted food to their pets. I too worried through the pet food scare and researched every morsel my cats consumed during the period of contamination. In reading the story *True Reflections*, I understood the need which compelled Sande Kay to share her own personally intimate True reflections.

Just as we are all born uniquely different, so are the felines that enter our lives. There are a thousand intimate moments which create the loving bond that exists between a cat and their person. Whether that feline is introduced as a small kitten or adopted as an adult, there are lessons to be learned by both as the relationship evolves. Time plays a great factor when bonding, as some relationships will simply taking longer than others. In circumstances of Universal intervention, it's the cat who displays great excitement of an instantaneous recognition when first encountering their new owner. Each relationship is an exceptional experience and as the stories in this book demonstrate, forms a spiritual bond between a cat and their person. In Mia and Catherine's story this became their experience as they reconnected in *Finding Karma at the SPCA*.

Discovering the idiosyncratic nature of your feline's personality is one of the more endearing aspects of a new relationship. The lessons of love coupled with the individuality of your union are distinctively personal. My kitten Caterina and I may have experienced a delay in bonding, but I will be eternally grateful for the Universal intervention which enabled our paths to cross. Upon our first meeting we failed to recognize each other, but to my great fortune she was simply the last Seal Point Himalayan female available in her breeder's cattery. As the years passed though, I have accepted this precious girl to be an extension of myself in the form of a cat;

for we grew to understand each other intimately and she will forever remain my Feline Soul Mate.

Some stories required hours of interviews, with days and weeks to complete them. Great care has been taken to ensure that I was respecting the unique bond shared between an owner and their cat. As these stories have originated from all over the world, to alter a phrase I believe would also alter the integrity of the story. Therefore whenever possible I have attempted to maintain the dialect of the cat owner because I believe much would be lost should their story not be written using their own words.

Readers have asked which of my personality traits best contributes to my writing. The answer is obvious, especially for those who know me well. "It's my sensitivity," I will respond, however I then feel compelled to admit that unfortunately that same sensitivity is also my greatest obstacle to overcome while writing. One roommate sadly confided that my preferences in both literature and movies were simply too heart warming for her tastes. The fact that she said this with the same expression as one sucking on a sour lemon was food for thought. Nevertheless to thine own self be true, for this is the essence of who I truly am.

You will also find a multitude of compelling cat quotes scattered throughout these pages. Emma, as featured in *The Mysterious Miss Kitty,* once gave me a small desk calendar filled with cat pictures and quotes. Until that time I wasn't aware of the many cat quotes that had been written by the famous and yet to be famous ailurophiles. As there are surely other feline lovers who have yet to be exposed to these wonderful quotes, they have been placed throughout this book when the words met the intention of the story. One particular favourite quote of mine is:

*Cats won't lie on a book that isn't well written.*
**- Harold Weiss**

I will never claim to have written a book that is completely free from grammatical errors; however this is a book that honours all cats. One reviewer, upon reading my first book, went so far as to claim that my love for cats "seeps through the pages." I was grateful for her insight for she identified the essence which is my personal truth and may become evident to you as the reader of these pages.

Therefore should your cat select this book to rest upon, I will then consider it a great compliment. For although it may not be due to my writing ability, possibly your cat will sense that a profound affection for felines resides within, and indeed seeps through the pages. My hope is that you will enjoy these stories, and may that enjoyment compensate grammatically for whatever may be missing.

*Perhaps cats and writers simply go together because*
*the cat is the perfect companion for the solitary, sedentary artist.*
**- Linda Sunshine**

# The Blue Angel & Her Garden of Pets
## - by Nick L. Sacco

*Anyone who has accustomed himself to regard the life*
*of any living creature as worthless is in danger of arriving also at*
*the idea of worthless human lives.*
**- Albert Schweitzer**

As volunteers with a cat rescue group, my wife and I have often shared our most celebrated success stories with others. An abandoned litter saved, a kitten finds the perfect "forever home," another nursed back to health from the brink of death.

Unfortunately, along with the many stories of success there are all too many stories of sadness. Sick cats left on a doorstep with little chance of survival, pets who have served much of their lives giving unconditional love only to be abandoned in shelters and on the streets, innocent unwanted creatures abused and neglected in innumerable and unfathomable ways. We watch too many of these broken hearted cats simply pine away and die; sad, alone, confused, wondering what they have done to deserve this fate.

A particular story comes to mind that is at once sad and inspiring. We had taken in an abandoned mother and her sick kittens that were no more than three weeks old. Despite our best efforts, within three days two of the three had died and by the third evening we knew the same inevitable fate would claim the last. Though serving my country as a Marine coupled with a career in law enforcement has toughened me in many ways, I tend to be a soft hearted person when it comes to these moments and I take the death of every kitten probably even harder than my wife who fights so hard to save them.

Late that night as I watched this kitten lie there nearly motionless in its cage, clinging to the last bit of life, I could just not bear the thought that this kitten would leave this world alone. I wrapped the dying kitten in something warm and cozy, and carried this precious baby up to bed with me and, keeping it cupped in my arm, lay down with it. The next hour seemed like an eternity as I prayed silently in the dark, listening to the baby struggle and fight for life, jerking every so often and letting out with a small, sad meow. I knew its life was ebbing away as these little gasps at life became fainter and weaker. In my prayers I repeatedly asked God, "What happens to the kittens when they die?" As a Christian I understand the concept of salvation and heaven, but I had to wonder about these innocents? What happens to them? Where do they go? What awaits them?

During my vigil of prayers, still holding this nearly lifeless kitten, I drifted off to peaceful slumber surrounded by my thoughts and prayers. I awoke sadly, immediately sensing the kitten was gone, but still feeling a presence of sorts filling the room. As I sat up and allowed my eyes to focus I was surprised to see a woman standing near me at the foot of my bed. What some may call a vision or a dream was as clear and real to me as anything I hold dear, and remains as clear to me today as when I first awoke. I felt no fear, only a sense of peace.

The woman appeared middle aged, with delicate features and chestnut hair that was parted in the middle and gathered in a bun. A flowing sash the warm color of blue sage was draped over her shoulders accenting her soft azure gown that billowed as if in a gentle breeze, though the air inside the room remained still and silent. I immediately knew in my heart that this must be an angel. Her smile instantly warmed me through to the depths of my soul as I paused for a moment to take it all in. I then realized that in her hands she was holding the small kitten who I had just held and comforted in its last moments of life not an hour before, the sad, empty shell of which still remained beside me on the bed. This small kitten of powder white innocence, however, was not the sickly, suffering, abandoned animal of a short while ago. Its coat was healthy and shined, blue eyes bright and clear, and it rolled and purred in the woman's hands in ways it never had the luxury of doing before.

The scene suddenly transformed and I found myself no longer within the confines of my own bedroom, but in the most beautiful garden eyes have ever seen. Birds and insects flew every which way; wonderfully fragrant flowers and trees of all sorts grew in every direction, as lush meadows and blue ponds of water dotted the landscape.

This "Blue Angel" sat watching my wonder and amazement from across a small brook and finally she began to speak. In a voice as soft as a harp's song she explained that she had been sent to me to answer the questions I had asked in my prayers that night. She told me how every living thing is equally important to God because they were created by his hand. Quoting the Bible she said, "Not a sparrow falls that God does not know about." She then said to me the thing that most struck my heart: "I am an Angel who has chosen to serve here in the Garden of the Pets by my own request." In an instant, without further explanation, I understood that every pet that dies goes to their own special garden where a truly special Angel awaits them. Together they will remain with the Angel, caring for, playing with and forever loving them until the day comes to pass that the pet's one and true human companion comes over to join them. "But what if a pet doesn't have a special human companion?" I asked, and the Angel simply replied, "Then we stay together here forever," she said smiling. As the scene began to fade, images surrounding the "Blue Angel" became apparent, images of many kittens and older cats. Some slept soundly; some played in the lush green meadow chasing butterflies and tackling each other; and as any proper cat must do, some groomed lazily in the sunlight. Many of the kittens I could recognize as ones who had touched my life in some way before they died, and in my last image of the "Blue Angel" I saw her place the little white kitten on the ground as her two siblings raced up to pounce excitedly upon their sister.

Since that time I've continued to have visits from the "Blue Angel" during my dreams. Often these visits come after the loss of a cat or kitten for which I held a close, personal affection. It's as if she wants to reassure me that all is well. It's a busy garden with the "Blue Angel" as I watch happy, healthy, beloved kittens run and play around her. I always awake with a feeling of inner peace knowing these babies will be there waiting for the day when my turn comes to meet with the "Blue Angel" and collect my cherished souls.

Each year there are still sad times that come along with all the good, and sadly there will always be kittens we can't save and each loss still hits me as hard as the last, but I smile inside knowing the "Blue Angel" awaits them. As I write down these thoughts I know a new kitten season is upon us and that many sick babies and lost souls are just beyond the horizon. Many kittens, like the one who first lead me to the "Blue Angel," will come into my life as theirs nears the end. I've adopted a firm belief that no kitten deserves to ever die alone, never knowing what it is to be loved. So when the end nears I'll wrap them up warm and safe and sit with them in my rocker. I'll hold them close and through the tears will softly whisper comforting stories of the Rainbow Bridge, the "Blue Angel" who is waiting for them in the meadow that lies before it, and the wonders that lie beyond. Eventually the end will come and they'll be laid to rest in my own personal garden of kittens behind our home, which, though quiet and peaceful is nowhere as beautiful as the garden to which their souls have already passed on.

Someday my journey in this life will also end and when given the choice I will proudly don my own robes in shades of blue, collect my kittens from the "Blue Angel" who has devoted her own afterlife to caring for them so that there will be more room for other souls to join her, and in peace become the caretaker of my own Garden of the Pets.

The Blue Angel & Her Garden of Pets

Nick L. Sacco and his wife Alisa live in Raytown, Missouri, and volunteer at the Kansas City Siamese Rescue:

**www.kcsiameserescue.org**

The painting on the preceding page was executed by artist Dave Marak of Kansas City. A full color rendition of this painting may be viewed at:

**www.ccbpublishing.com/blueangel.html**

Dave Marak works with Kansas City Animal Control and is a close friend of the Kansas City Siamese Rescue group. Additional examples of Dave Marak's work may be viewed at:

**www.kcsiameserescue.org/davemarak.html**

The author may be contacted directly by e-mail at:

**mr.marine@comcast.net**

# My Cat is So Insolent, She Has A Price on Her Head

## - by Robin Doll

*Cats are cool. They have style, personality, sophistication,*
*and just the right amount of confidence.*
**- Michael Bolton**

Where to begin – I got Honey when she was half-grown; she was the last of the litter that a friend's cat had had. I just told her to drop the little darling off while I was bagging groceries for minimum wage. This was eleven years ago. I came home from my job at Albertson's and my Mom said, "Robin, there's a wild cat somewhere in this house. I want you to find it and take care of it. I can't get within ten feet of the little beast." I found the "beast" under the spare bed that my brother used to use until he left for college.

She had the most feral, mistrusting eyes I'd ever seen! I thought she was beautiful though. I could see that she had mostly black fur with white feet, a white bib and a splotch of white on her muzzle. I had to grab her when she refused to come out on her own and she slipped through my hands like quicksilver. Luckily I'd closed the door so she, in her fervent desire to escape ran straight into it. Poor kitty. I cradled her in my lap and stroked her little head, cooing that she was "mine forever." She just looked at me as if to say, "Shut up."

She got her name after I had moved to Boise and my roommate, Cyndi, heard me calling her Honey all the time. I also called her Baby and Sweetie but Honey seemed to stick and soon everyone called her that.

About a year later I had a so-so evening with my boyfriend and he was already on his way to work when I went outside and found my cat, Honey, crying on the sidewalk, having been shot twice. She was holding up one of her white paws, blood hitting the pavement in penny-sized drops. I looked at her, instantly regretful that I had let her out. She bothered me all day to give her some freedom and I figured it wouldn't hurt to let her go out and enjoy the sunshine while I had some quality time with Henry. "Well, go on then," I had said pettishly, holding the screen door open. She looked back at me with her green-yellowy eyes and I almost changed my mind, then she climbed over the fence and was off through the weeds. I spent the day dusting and scrubbing floors, and then Henry came back from visiting his parents. I forgot all about Honey, having let her out for whole days since I acquired her so many years ago. After tons of false alarms when I patrolled the many neighborhoods I lived in, only to find her up a tree or atop someone's tool shed, I figured she knew enough to stay off the road.

I scooped her up and ran upstairs. I put her down and tweaked her leg and it just hung there with her paw curled beneath her. She just glared at me, telling me that professional care was required at once, the expensive sort. Honey was debiting my bank account with her eyes. After grabbing a novel for the waiting room, I packed her into her pet taxi and we were off. It had to be serious, since she was too upset to stick her paws out of the holes in the door to her carrier.

We were at the clinic for a good two hours. I spent a king's ransom on x-rays alone. Her leg was broken, just as I feared. The x-rays revealed that she had been shot with a pellet gun; once in her right shoulder and once in her abdomen. I stood there in the examination room, staring at the ghostly image of Honey's skeleton on the wall. "Someone shot my cat?" I whispered. The doctor nodded and said that this was happening all the time. He went on to say that both pellets exited, and the stomach wound was minor as that pellet just grazed the fat pad. Some metal fragments were visible in the shoulder area, but luckily her internal organs were spared. The doctor assured me that Honey would live, but that she might lose the leg.

They don't do fracture repairs at the emergency clinic, so I would have to take her to a regular vet on Monday. I drove her back home in a daze and spent the weekend touching her paw at the end of her pink-bandaged leg, making her flex her claws. I saw a marathon of *America's Next Top Model* and cried along whenever another girl was cut from the herd. Then someone would call and get the bad news. "Do you want to watch obscure films and eat some Baklava?" "Oh, no thank you. I'd rather watch girls bawl in front of hard-faced judges and try to stimulate Honey's leg." It was a weekend to remember.

I found a vet who told me he could save her leg, and learned how to squirt medicine into my cat's mouth twice daily. All my friends know how much I adore my cat. When I was telling Cyndi about Honey being shot we were on the phone and we were both crying. I think that each and every one of my friends breathed a sigh of relief when they found out that she wasn't going to be an amputee.

Shortly thereafter Henry moved out; I had known since Memorial Day that it was only a matter of time and circumstance. I painted the apartment, and took Honey to the vet at insane hours of the morning. This whole experience shot a sliver of "pissed-off" into my demeanor. I work in customer service for a prominent satellite television company and sometimes while trying to explain billing to someone with a passel of brats squalling in the background, I wanted to throw my headset across the room. Luckily, I get free television service as one of my perks so when I was too poor to go out I still had syndicated cartoons to watch.

I used to put baby bonnets on Honey during parties, to her chagrin. I have photos of her sporting New Year's Eve tiaras as well. Last Halloween I got her a witch outfit at the dollar store and managed to get the pointy hat on her but she drew the line at donning the cape.

Honey in her witch outfit during Halloween

Today, it's like it never happened. She had to wear a pin in her shoulder for two months, but Honey has regained full use of her leg. She hates loud noises even more than she used to, but I can live with that. Usually I don't even think of how I once dropped a thousand dollars to have her put back together. I still daydream of finding the culprit, just so I could send him, or her, a picture of Honey with a note saying something like: ***"You missed!"***

# The Kitten's Choice
## - by Jasmine Kinnear

*Four little Persians, but only one looked in my direction.*
*I extended a tentative finger and two soft paws clung to it. There*
*was a contented sound of purring, I suspect on both our parts.*
- George Freedley

During my years of breeding and feline consulting I have met literally hundreds, if not thousands of people. From those purchasing my kitten books to others who have passed through my cattery, they all share one objective: to locate their own Feline Soul Mate.

It remains a mystery why one kitten will be selected over another. As a breeder I've witnessed several cases of love at first sight for both the kitten and their buyer. Although it may appear a simple matter of chance coupled with good timing, I believe there is Universal intervention involved. While selling litters I've always been able to identify the difference between those seeking their Feline Soul Mate from another only desiring the presence of a kitten in their home.

I have seen buyers overwhelmed when attempting to select their ideal kitten in a room full of identically coloured babies. Some buyers are so totally focused on a single colour or sex that they totally neglect to consider the kitten's personality.

I must confess though that this is precisely how I chose my own Feline Soul Mate, my precious Himalayan Caterina. I was totally focused on buying a

Seal Point female and in all honesty, it wasn't love at first sight for either of us. However within several hours of her presence in my home, I quickly realized how blessed I had been. She was the last kitten available, the only female and the only Seal Point Himalayan mature enough to leave her cattery. In retrospect it was Universal intervention that she became my cat and throughout her life we shared a profound emotional connection.

It is always a delight to meet former buyers many years later in chance encounters. However they usually recognize me, as I wasn't blessed with a good memory for recalling either people's names or faces. Strangely enough though, I rarely forget my many purebred kittens, and in chance encounters I'm able to quickly recall the names given to them by their new owners.

Such an unexpected meeting occurred some months ago while I was making a deposit at the bank. I had just bought a large bag of cat food and placed it on the counter while I was speaking to the young woman serving me. She mentioned that she loved cats too and we shared a few words of feline fancy.

"What kind of cat do you have?" I asked.

"A Himalayan male," she replied.

As with any true breeder, I inquired from which cattery she'd purchased her kitten. I was interested as I had once specialized in Himalayans in my own breeding program.

She couldn't recall the name of the cattery where she'd made the purchase however she mentioned the breeder lived in my area of the city.

"I just love him," she gushed. "Honestly, I've never owned such a special cat before. It's rather an unusual story because he was the one who really picked me."

She smiled fondly reflecting on the moment before continuing, "The breeder had a younger litter of Blue Persians and several older Himalayan babies that were also available. I was a little overwhelmed because there were kittens everywhere and I couldn't make a decision on which one was right for me. The breeder told me to take my time and come back in a few days which I thought was rather considerate. I decided that she was probably right and reached for my purse to leave. And there, tucked inside, was this adorable kitten sound asleep. I thought it must be fate and that he had to be the right one; truthfully I've never regretted my decision."

Gina's kitten, Sebastian

I stared at her in disbelief. Although I didn't recognize her, she had purchased that kitten from me over ten years before. I then provided her with the names of his mother and father including the name she had given her kitten. I remembered her shear delight in discovering Sebastian sleeping in her purse which had been left open in the viewing room.

Gina had gently removed him from her purse and I left them

alone to privately bond and cuddle together. So many years before she had been convinced that he was the right kitten, and time had proven her instincts correct. Sebastian had been a gentle kitten produced from one of my favourite breeding pairs, Tara and Honey. I was well acquainted with the personalities of their kittens and Gina nodded in agreement when I provided her with a basic personality profile of Sebastian as a mature feline.

"How do you know so much about him?" she asked a little puzzled. To which I replied, "His personality profile was outlined in my last published book. He was one of the foundation kittens which I profiled in my Felines by Design series."

We had forgotten each other over time, but had reconnected over a large bag of cat food.

"He's the best cat I've ever owned," she said proudly, and thanked me again for bringing her Feline Soul Mate into her life.

Several days later while once again in the bank, I left a signed copy of my book for Gina in which Sebastian's personality had been profiled. Although our paths have yet to cross again I knew one day I would be including her special story in this book. The inscription I wrote within her book read:

*"To Gina and Sebastian, may your lives continue to be blessed by many more chance meetings… Always, Jasmine."*

# The Cat in the Woods
## - by Jasmine Kinnear

*Cats are like greatness: Some people are born into cat-loving families, some achieve cats, and some have cats thrust upon them.*
- **William H. A. Carr**

In my government office I was known as the resident cat lover. My passion for felines didn't escape many as my work station was tastefully decorated with assorted cat memorabilia. My expertise in solving cat problems circulated through the office and so commenced the blossoming of my feline therapy practice. I enjoyed and became accustomed to those colleagues with feline issues seeking my counsel during office hours.

I was working in the staff lounge one morning arranging material for employees when Susy came in to start the coffee. Although we usually avoided each other's company, we always maintained an aura of professional decorum. This week it was Susy's turn to keep the lounge in order, so I knew she would be in the room for a while. I had a time sensitive task to complete and decided it was best to remain even though once being in Susy's company I was always left feeling inferior.

Susy was divorced and had an eight-year-old daughter whom she saw several times a year. She preferred the social life of a single person, and had given up custody of her daughter to the child's father. She was an attractive woman who loved fast cars, fast men, exotic vacations and the bar scene. We shared little in common as I was sensitive and engrossed in a conflict between furthering my career or finally having children of my own.

I thought at the time that Susy had probably made the right decision as she often appeared limited in compassion towards others in the office. To give up an only child was an incomprehensible act to me, however with age comes wisdom. As the years have passed and I've experienced more of life, I now have a better understanding of her parental decision. Susy was wise enough to know her personal limitations and that maternal self-sacrifice was not within her nature.

She was busy for a few minutes and then turned to face me. She hesitated for several seconds before she spoke, as if showing concern that she may be disturbing me. As I now recall, this was the only time in the three years we'd worked together that she'd ever initiated a conversation.

"I had something strange happen to me this weekend," she began, "and I thought you might be able to tell me what it all meant."

I realized she was actually troubled and indicated that I wanted to listen. As the coffee brewed she came over and started helping me compile stacks of paper into completed files. She was not known to enjoy working and freely volunteering like this was definitely out of character.

She started by saying that she and her boyfriend had just returned from a camping trip over the long weekend. About an hour before they had planned to return home her boyfriend left the campsite to load their van. Susy was relaxing and smoking a cigarette, sitting with her back against a large tree when something unexpected happened.

Speaking quietly she said, "I heard a noise behind me and turned to see this skinny cat a few feet away. The cat and I stared at each other for a few moments and then it began crying loudly. I turned away and tried to ignore it for several minutes. I was hoping it would get the message that I'm not a 'cat person' and just get lost." Susy did not want to become involved and definitely was not in the mood to rescue someone's lost pet.

The cat's howling intensified, forcing Susy's attention back to the feline again. Finally she fished through her backpack searching for the last of their weekend rations. Opening a small tin of luncheon meat, she reluctantly rose to her feet and placed it a short distance from the thin, desolate cat. The feline watched her cautiously but always remained at a safe distance. Susy could see that the cat was starving as she drooled just from the scent of the meat. Nourishment however was not the tabby's immediate concern. The feral cat ignored Susy's offering and continued howling and pacing in circles around the food.

After several minutes Susy realized the cat was trying to communicate something distressful, so she decided to follow her into the forest. Together they made their way through the thick woods for a considerable distance. Susy was not only curious but also sensed the cat's desperation as the feral continually turned to make sure she was still being followed. The tabby made her way towards an abandoned log cabin where she jumped onto a tree branch lying next to the house.

Nearing the cabin, Susy could hear the frantic sound of starving kittens coming from beneath the house and realized the cat's desperate plight. There had been a windstorm several days before and perhaps the mother had left the litter to hunt for food. In her absence, a tree had fallen across the entrance separating the mother from her young litter.

The feral cat remained on the tree branch as Susy leaned over the tree beside her. She had just enough room to reach under the house to pull out one kitten after another. Susy commented that the mother cat was making strange noises while the babies fearlessly came to her outstretched hand, one at a time to be lifted up to safety. During those moments Susy shared an emotional experience with this feral mother and her kittens.

When Susy had rescued the last baby, she watched as the litter of five scrawny kittens gathered around their mother. Susy dished out the luncheon meat she'd brought with her and watched as the small, starving brood quickly consumed it. The tabby queen carefully watched over her kittens and although she was probably starving herself, never touched any of the meat.

Susy stood a few feet away, watching in amazement that any cat could communicate with a human in such a manner as this feral mother had just demonstrated with her. She said the queen quietly stared at her, blinking her eyes several times, and then swiftly left with the babies following behind. When Susy returned to the campsite she confided to her boyfriend that it was an experience she'd never forget.

Susy shared this touching story of a mother's devotion with me over thirty years ago. However what I noticed were the changes in Susy's priorities following that encounter with the cat in the woods. After that day I never saw Susy in quite the same manner as I had before. She appeared to be a little less self-involved and seemed to show more consideration towards others. Something about that feral encounter in the woods had changed her. Several weeks later she confessed that she had adopted a tabby kitten from the local shelter.

As my knowledge of feline behaviour increased, I came to understand much of what the feral cat was trying to communicate to Susy. In retrospect it now also makes sense why Susy was the person selected by the feral queen. Other people had been camping in the area but the mother specifically wanted only Susy to help save her litter. Perhaps someone else would have trapped the feline family in an attempt to rescue them from such a difficult life. The tabby seemed to realize that Susy would help her but not interfere with the litter's feral existence.

The kittens had never been near a human before and should have been more fearful. The mother, however, communicated to each kitten by purr name to ignore the offensive human odour and permit Susy to lift them to safety. The wild tabby communicated her gratitude to Susy by blinking her eyes, to thank her for giving assistance and providing food to her starving litter. Susy sensed that the mother was trying to communicate her gratitude and instinctively understood because she was also a mother.

When Susy first shared this sad story with me I was initially concerned that the litter had been left in the wild to manage on their own. However Susy felt she had done what she was asked to do, and seemed comfortable with her decision to let the litter wander away. Had I been there that day the feral mother would never have approached me. Somehow she must have sensed Susy's true nature, her ability to separate her feelings, to have enough compassion to help without interfering with the litter's feral existence. I now understand that Susy did the right thing by simply listening to the mother's needs and responding as she did.

*Cats are intended to teach us*
*that not everything in nature has a purpose.*
**- Garrison Keillor**

It also warmed my heart to know that Susy finally found a loving feline companion. After she became a cat owner I noticed two small pictures appear on her desk, one of her new tabby kitten and one of her daughter.

I'd like to believe that Susy's experience with the cat in the woods triggered her own maternal instincts. Sharing the mother cat's love for her kittens and her courage to overcome fear and starvation truly touched Susy's heart. She may have physically helped the feral cat, but another exchange had also taken place between the two mothers. Susy was finally ready to begin the emotional journey back into her own daughter's heart.

I was not the only person in our office who recognized the subtle changes in Susy. However I was the one person with whom she shared the reasons behind those changes. Only another cat lover could comprehend the importance of such a simple miracle. Susy's life and priorities had shifted due to an unexpected feline encounter during that long weekend. She had been touched by the maternal love of a tabby feral mother caring for her starving litter trapped in the woods; and Susy alone had made a difference.

*Way down deep, we're all motivated by the same urges.*
*Cats have the courage to live by them.*
**- Jim Davis**

# The Ugliest Cat
## - by Esther Sustersich

*Introduction by Jasmine Kinnear…*

It is a privilege when I encounter cat owners willing to share personal stories about their felines. I am drawn to the devotion of such owners as their warm stories have taken shape over the span of many years. However these tales can only be fully appreciated when they have been written with the loving sincerity of their owners. *The Ugliest Cat* demonstrates the substance within the relationship of a woman and her feline. Such stories will surface in the most unlikely of places and will be shared under some unexpected circumstances.

Esther shared her story of *The Ugliest Cat* as we stood shivering in the early morning cold in a long queue of book lovers. On the first weekend in March our local newspaper holds a gigantic sale of donated books with the proceeds assisting local schools in our community. The Times Colonist Book Sale attracts many of Vancouver Island's book lovers who, in great anticipation, will spend many cold hours waiting in line for the chance to discover a buried treasure.

This is an annual event that remains near and dear to my heart and come rain or shine I never miss it. Even the simple act of standing in line and being in the presence of other book lovers is always an exhilarating experience. Every year the newspaper must locate a massive facility that is transformed into a makeshift bookstore containing thousands of reasonably priced books for sale. The event has also become a magnet for those seeking a book that has been out of circulation for years. I am not only a writer but also dearly love the printed word and own a treasured collection of signed books. This year I was seeking not only to increase my collection of Royalty and biography books but also valuable research books in my continuing study of felines.

Although the doors do not open until 9:00 a.m. people have been known to camp out overnight or arrive before dawn to be first in line. My husband and I must travel for this great event and usually take our place in line about ninety minutes prior to the grand opening.

While my husband parked the car I took a place in line and listened to the conversations around me. The couple in front claimed to have read all the books they purchased last year with the final book just finished the week before this year's sale. Behind me I listened to the warm conversation between two girlfriends while waiting for my husband to return.

Clutching my coffee cup in an attempt to warm my hands, I watched a domestic cat sitting in the window of her home. She was obviously curious about the long line of book lovers in front of her house. The women behind me laughed whenever a dog would appear beside the cat to look through the curtains, equally entertained by so many people. I remarked to my husband that the cat probably thought we had been placed in line for her entertainment. There is something special about people who love pets and even more so those who equally share a love for the printed word. My feline comment began a conversation with the women behind us and we shared a mutual affection for our cats who were patiently waiting for our arrival back home.

Esther and Lucy shared a lifelong friendship and also enjoyed a common interest in books. Esther confessed to having travelled from Courtenay, a small community many miles away to enjoy the book sale. She was staying with Lucy during her visit and had travelled to Victoria specifically to partake in this annual event.

Esther, unaware that I was a writer of feline material, spoke with loving affection about her beloved cat Bowie. The circumstances surrounding Bowie's appearance in her life were so important that she confessed to having written a story regarding his timely arrival on her doorstep.

It is my belief that when we are selected by a feline the relationship holds a greater meaning, even more so in the case of Esther and Bowie, whose unexpected meeting was Universally predestined.

*Esther's story...*

The doorbell rang one evening and upon answering it there stood Mike, one of the children who lived on our street. He was holding a scrawny black and white kitten that looked about three months old.

Mike said, "I have your cat here. He was by my house, so I thought I'd bring him over."

"That's not Whiskee," I said. "He's exactly the same colour but Whiskee doesn't have one blue eye and one green eye." I thanked him, closed the door and said to my husband, "Have you ever seen an uglier cat?"

We didn't give the little kitten another thought that evening. However the next morning when I went outside, the kitten was sitting at the bottom of the stairs. I picked him up so we could take him to the SPCA later that day. As soon as he was in my arms he started to purr like crazy. That was it. There was no way I was taking this kitty to an animal shelter. My husband didn't want to let him stay though because we already had a cat.

"But we have to keep him," I insisted. "He's so ugly no one will want him. They will put him to sleep."

Thankfully it was the weekend and our local SPCA was closed. My husband said I could feed him but that he was not allowed in the house. I gave him some food, which he gobbled down and then threw up a few minutes later. Concerned, I called the vet about it. He said it was probably just because he ate so quickly, and I should feed him a small amount of food at a time. I did so and he was fine.

Esther, Whiskee and Bowie

By the next day this young stray had managed to make it into the house. Later that evening while we were sitting on the patio, he saw a reflection of himself in the patio door and pounced at it. Hitting his head against the glass door he became somewhat dazed but was otherwise unharmed; except maybe for his ego. My husband could only shake his head at the kitten's antics. Shortly thereafter this stray kitten had a name – Bowie – named after David Bowie, who also has two different coloured eyes.

Bowie officially became part of our family and just like our other cat, Whiskee, was allowed to go anywhere he wanted. Whiskee was a sweet older female we'd owned for several years but she was *not* impressed with Bowie. She started to sulk almost immediately so we gave her some extra attention and figured she would get over it.

Everyone who met Bowie was amazed at how similar the two cats looked. The only way to tell them apart, other than by size, was the colour of their eyes and one small black mark on Bowie's face.

Bowie

Over the next few days and weeks Whiskee continued to sulk and spend more and more time outside under a bush, while Bowie explored his new home. Whenever we brought them together Bowie would harass Whiskee by chasing her tail or pouncing on her, trying to get her to play. Whiskee just laid there looking at him. When Whiskee went to eat, Bowie would run up and try to play with her. We had to place Bowie in another part of the house so Whiskee could at least eat in peace. While they may not have been best friends, we were glad that they were not fighting.

However after a few weeks we started getting concerned because Whiskee seemed unhappy all the time. We took her to the vet and to our shock learned that she was suffering from severe kidney failure and nothing could be done for her. We felt so guilty because we did not realize the difference between being sick and being resentful of our new kitten.

When Whiskee died we were heartbroken. However it was a bit easier to deal with because Bowie was there to comfort us. Everyone told us that it was as if Bowie knew we were going to need him soon, and that's why he came back to our house after Mike had first brought him here. There is no doubt in my mind that this is true.

Bowie is now ten years old and I am thankful everyday that he is in our lives. Unlike the first time I saw him and said he was an ugly cat, I now tell him each and every day that he is the most beautiful kitty in the world.

> *What greater gift than the love of a cat?*
> **- Charles Dickens**

*Conclusion by Jasmine Kinnear...*

For a short time the kitten remained nameless until Esther's husband, Jim, accepted the miniature odd eyed version of Whiskee. Esther explained that without prior discussion they had each decided on the same name for their new kitten. It is my belief that it was actually Bowie who selected Esther and Jim. He may have appeared as a stray kitten at their front door but he had always been predestined to be their feline. In so doing, his presence in their lives lessened the shock of Whiskee's unexpected death.

Ten years later Esther remains mystified why a small kitten mirroring Whiskee's identical colouring would appear just before her only female cat died.

Bowie has a medical condition that separates him from other felines and he remains a medical mystery even to his veterinarian. His blood work is never quite normal and he has been known to grow non-malignant tumours on his body. Esther mentioned that her vet simply accepts that Bowie is an unusual cat and often says, "I keep on having to remind myself that this is Bowie."

The circumstances around Bowie's timely arrival, the spontaneous selection of his name and the identical colouring of both felines were so unusual that Esther's friends believed she should write his story. I agreed with her and she proudly announced that his story had already been written. She promised to forward it for consideration in the first volume of *Every Cat Has A Story*. Esther's devotion for her beautiful Bowie is a story that needs to be acknowledged.

How fortunate for Esther that she saw so much beauty in an ugly stray kitten. For the last ten years she has thanked the Universe for providing her with the gift of her beautiful boy. Bowie has grown into a lovely male but perhaps his beauty has been intensified by Esther's daily message that he is indeed the most beautiful kitty in the world.

There are some who will scoff at the concept that everything happens within our lives for a reason. This however remains my preference in accepting many of the events I have encountered in my own life. Was it simply chance that a lost kitten would be found on the doorstep of a home mirroring a feline who would shortly be dying? Was it simply a matter of chance that Esther would take her place in a line of strangers only to be standing behind another cat lover? A cat lover working on a book containing stories of unusual feline encounters such as Esther had written? Had the beautiful domestic feline perched on the windowsill observing the queue of people in line not been so endearing would I have mentioned her presence? Perhaps as the reader of this story you are meant to one day also recognize a kitten that has been born and has been placed specifically to add a greater meaning to your life. Maybe you have also known a feline that was uniquely special to you and equally deserves recognition. Every cat does indeed have a story, and their life also deserves to be acknowledged, written and published for other cat lovers to enjoy.

# Finding Karma at the SPCA

*Getting a cat is a greater commitment than getting married.*
**- Seymour and Paula Chwast**

This story is taken from Jasmine Kinnear's Feline Forum on her Confessions of a Cat Breeder web site:
www.confessionsofacatbreeder.com

*Catherine writes…*

Okay, this is my story…

Yesterday after work I went out for a drive in the country with Maggie, my adopted Greyhound. However I got caught in traffic at the tunnel on my way back home. Rather than sit in line, I got off the main road and decided to follow the river hoping I would come across another route back.

As I was driving, I saw an SPCA sign. I followed it and ended up at the SPCA's door. I got out and went in to see the cats. There was this beautiful Chocolate Point Siamese; she was a rescue from a "cat mill" breeder with 39 others. They divided them up between shelters and she was the last one to go at this one. She hadn't been handled much and was very shy. I asked if I could hold her but was warned that she did not like to cuddle. Yet she took to me like a fish to water. The woman at the shelter who was with me said that she was going to find out more information. Then another person appeared and a moment later yet another person appeared. They all commented on how much this cat was "taking" to me. It was instant karma; I knew I wasn't leaving without her.

The second lady told me that she had been adopted out, but that woman brought her back because of "allergies" two days ago, after only having the cat for about a week. The woman told them that she didn't like being held, nor did she cuddle, yet insisted it was because of her "allergies" that she was being brought back. Apparently I was the first person who "the cat" had let touch and hold her like this. I knew the second I held her it was meant to be.

So now I have a new cat. Maggie has been great but she had never really heard a cat cry before, and was quite thrown aback and became excited about it. "The cat" has been great with Maggie and hasn't hissed or anything. They have been really quite cute together.

We went to see our vet today; she is about two years old and is 5.5 lbs. She won't get much bigger, she might fill out a little more, but that's it. She is very shy and likes to either sleep on my chest or hide under the covers in a box. The vet said this will change. Look at what she has been through. She has lived in a cage for most of her life, has never had a name, and within the last little while she has been either at the SPCA, the vet's office or that first adoptee's house.

The problem is, as I'm sure you have noticed, that I haven't come up with a name for her yet. This is where you come in. Please help! I need names, I need ideas. What do you think? I'm really having a tough time coming up with one.

She has already changed my life but I really need a great name for her, and any other suggestions to help her in this transition. I'm hoping to get a photo soon, but until then she looks like a Siamese with chocolate and cafe au lait markings/colours, and her eyes are very deep blue.

You can e-mail me for a further response if you want to make it brief here in this forum.

Thanks in advance for your advice,

Catherine

*Jasmine's Reply...*

Dear Catherine,

Thank you for submitting your question. I appreciate the opportunity to address several important issues that your situation presents.

I believe that few are fortunate in finding their Feline Soul Mate during their lives. Even professional breeders encountering many cats are not subject to the fortune of discovering their own Feline Soul Mate despite having an extended breeding career.

By trusting your instincts I believe that you and your Chocolate Point Siamese were reunited. A sure indication of this is the great joy that she displayed during your initial meeting. She simply recognized you, and with astute intuition you realized that she was meant to be in your life.

Often a shy or reserved cat will become quite anxious to be held, with the chosen individual experiencing a 'karmic' feeling that this chance meeting was simply meant to be. This appears to have been your experience as well. The SPCA staff member was shocked at the female's reaction to your presence as she had previously shown little desire to be held by anyone else.

Shortly after posting your inquiry on the Feline Forum I received an e-mail indicating your selection of a name for your little girl. Your chosen name of 'Mia' for your queen is quite ideal. I will therefore use Mia's new name as I continue your consultation.

I believe that Mia is a soul whom you have loved before. Often these special felines are more sensitive to past life connections and are the first to recognize us. I truly envy the years ahead for your relationship to develop and mature. I believe you will find this relationship to be an especially close and rewarding one. Mia will understand you on a level that you may never have encountered before. There will be times when you may wonder if she could be telepathically reading your thoughts. Should you return home stressed from a difficult day she may become quite demanding, insisting that you relax and take time to pet her. When you are depressed or not feeling well she may shadow your movements and stay close by to provide her comfort and support. Her love will be constant, unconditional, and she will become a living blessing working within your life.

Despite my great affinity for cats, I have experienced my own Feline Soul Mate but once during my life. As was the Universal plan, it was a matter of chance that I found her and precisely at a time when her presence was essential for my well-being. After 13 years of sharing our lives she crossed to the Rainbow Bridge on October 1st, 1998. Despite the number of felines I presently treasure and love, my relationship with my Feline Soul Mate could never be duplicated. I will always carry an emptiness within me that only she could fill.

Years ago as a novice breeder, not following my inherited good senses, I purchased three felines sick with ringworm. One was a ten-month-old white Persian female. She had lived a totally caged existence and never experienced freedom. She attempted to show her desire for affection however became fearful whenever I interacted with her. I sensed her desire to respond and knew only too well the depth of her loneliness and sense of abandonment. I was totally drawn to her and slowly attempted to regain her trust. I began with changing her name from Danaluk to Dana. By working within her emotional restrictions she eventually trusted enough to leave the confinements of her self-imposed caged life. I was finally able to bond with her and she became one of the foundation queens in my cattery.

Dana

I owned her for several years but always believed she deserved to become a beloved pet. It was during those years that my dear friend Judy was also passing through a difficult period in her own life. Instinctively, I knew that Judy was the right person for this lovely Persian queen. Now, years later, I believe my instincts were correct and Dana has brought Judy great contentment. With Judy's loving care this little female is extremely affectionate and totally devoted to her mistress. She loves her mother's lap and at times is demanding when she believes her dinner should be served. There is no greater reward than to watch a once fearful cat blossom and flourish within the right environment. You will also notice this gradual change in Mia's personality with the passing of time. I am sure you are already sensing a natural rhythm and flow to your relationship.

Maggie did not sense Mia to be just another cat as you both projected the same familiar flow of energy. As you and Maggie have an established and loving relationship, Mia was also not fearful in Maggie's presence. The relationship between both your dog and cat was a comfortable transition as each accepted the other as a loving projection of their mistress.

The importance of a feline's name should never be underestimated. You were wise to provide Mia with some time in assisting you to select a comfortable name for her. My advice to owners is to never capitalize on a negative aspect of their cat's personality when deciding on a name. A cat given a skittish name will surely remain skittish. A troublesome cat with a rambunctious name will likewise live up to the energy that name implies.

A cat with a troubled past such as Mia's will eventually re-name themselves after living within a new environment. Many felines will completely accept a loving owner, thereby leaving the negative energy of their old life behind. The name Mia is a soft, endearing name indicating "Beloved cat of mine" and "My cat, a part of myself." How appropriate, as now she is loved by you.

Perhaps Mia's first adoption was unsuccessful due to her inability to socialize. However I prefer to believe that it was Universal intervention. The "allergies" were simply a part of the Universal plan for Mia to be in the right place to claim you as her rightful owner at exactly the right time.

I would be interested in learning how you selected her lovely name because it is most appropriate. I have a theory about such situations and I am curious as to whether it proves correct in your case. Will you please let me know?

Once again, thank you Catherine for your wonderful story. It always warms my heart when an owner and cat are reunited as you have been with Mia.

Best wishes,

Jasmine

51

*Another cat? Perhaps.*
*For love there is also a season; its seeds must be re-sown.*
*But a family cat is not replaceable like a worn out coat or a set*
*of tires. Each new kitten becomes its own cat, and none is*
*repeated. I am four cats old, measuring out my life in friends*
*that have succeeded but not replaced one another.*
**- Irving Townsend**

*Catherine's story continues…*

It's now September 25th, and on October 8th it will be two months that Mia and I have been together.

She is my *fourth* cat since I became an adult and the seventh cat in my life since I was 7 years old. What I didn't tell you was that a couple of weeks before I found Mia, my beloved boy Dave passed away in my arms at 1:30 am on July 27th. He had just turned twenty. I found him at the Vancouver SPCA in November 1981, while looking for a lost dog that belonged to my boss.

Mia is still very shy; however she has started to come out of the bedroom within the last week. I share my home with a friend, and Mia only comes out when no one is around. She still doesn't like being picked up but after a game of hide and seek under the bed she will give in. She continues to like hiding under a blanket on my lap when we are in the living room. But mostly she takes off like a bat out of hell and wants to explore and not be touched.

She plays a lot with her toys and Maggie's too. At first she would only play with them when we were out but now she plays with them in front of both me and the dog. I lost my cell phone last week, only to find it under the bed up near the headboard surrounded by her toys.

When I first brought her home it took her days to purr, and now she's so loud it wakes me up. She wouldn't sleep with me at all but after a week or so, she now gets on the bed; only when I'm almost asleep does she get as close as she can to my neck and shoulder. She also gives me kisses on my face regularly. Last week was the first time she did the kneading thing against my neck. A couple of days later she climbed into bed, curled up against me and started to lick my ear. Dave and Cleo used to do that to each other all the time; Cleo passed away in 1996 when she was 15 years old.

Last Friday night I was up rather late when Mia started running around the house like crazy, just because she could. She even started doing that wiggle, the hind legs thing, before she took off. Now if I'm home and don't open the door to my room right away, she cries. Whenever Maggie and I leave she sits in the bedroom window and watches us get into the car. When I get home she starts as I'm walking up the stairs.

She also rubs herself against the dog's face, back and forth every morning, and sometimes before bed. Mia has even tripped me from under the bed and she plays with Maggie from under there too, batting her legs and face. Once in a while if Maggie gets too rambunctious with her, she will hiss.

All in all things are coming along fine, slowly but surely. She only acts like a cat when no one other than myself is around. She is still taking it very slow with my roommate and her boyfriend, as well as anyone else who visits.

As for her name, I was going to call her Tess, but I wasn't sure, and I got negative feedback. So I started to look up different web sites. I was drawn to the letter "M" then I saw Mia. I'm still not sure if it's her. I've called her Tess, Muffin, Tasha, Mika… I still don't know.

Well that's it for now. Thank you for writing back to me.

Regards,

Catherine

I am going to identify Mia's response to Catherine's loving and devoted care from the perspective of a Feline Behaviour Consultant.

Catherine describes, *"She continues to like hiding under a blanket on my lap when we are in the living room."*

Mia's prior life was a lonely confined caged existence. Although such a life is emotionally harmful for a breeding queen, the space restriction also provides alternate levels of frustration and a sense of security. Mia's preference for lying on Catherine's lap with the protection of a blanket mirrors the intimacy she shared with her mother as a kitten.

In Catherine's words, *"Last Friday night I was up rather late when Mia started running around the house like crazy, just because she could. She even started doing that wiggle, the hind legs thing, before she took off. Now if I'm home and don't open the door to my room right away, she cries."*

Catherine has permitted Mia the freedom of choice. Felines who explore their home with such energy, exhibiting the hind leg bunny jumping reflex are reflecting their love and the great joy they are experiencing in their environment.

*"When I first brought her home it took her days to purr, and now she's so loud it wakes me up. She wouldn't sleep with me at all but after a week or so, she now gets on the bed; only when I'm almost asleep does she get as close as she can to my neck and shoulder. She also gives me kisses on my face regularly. Last week was the first time she did the kneading thing against my neck. A couple of days later she climbed into bed, curled up against me and started to lick my ear. Dave and Cleo used to do that to each other all the time; Cleo passed away in 1996 when she was 15 years old."*

Mia has accepted Catherine as her Mom; the gradual purr, the cuddling next to her mistress' neck and shoulders are familiar to this feline since the last loving contact she experienced was sleeping with her mother and littermates in this fashion. The 'kneading thing' against Catherine's neck is called "Milktreading" and was associated with Mia nursing as a kitten from her mother. A cat will perform this act at a very slow pace of approximately one stroke every two seconds. As Catherine has mentioned, Mia will always accompany this procedure with loud purring.

*"She also rubs herself against the dog's face, back and forth every morning, and sometimes before bed. Mia has even tripped me from under the bed and she plays with Maggie from under there too, batting her legs and face. Once in a while if Maggie gets too rambunctious with her, she will hiss."*

Mia is implementing a scent-exchange between herself and Maggie by rubbing herself against the dog's face every morning. Mia is marking 'her dog' with those special scent glands located on her temples and at the gaps of her mouth. Mia is actually reading both Catherine's and Maggie's scent signals when she is cleaning herself. She is literally tasting them both with her tongue. Mia's routine has special meanings... she has accepted her family and has demonstrated her affection by routinely scent-exchanging with them and identifying their scent as a part of her accepted family.

Catherine's posting on our Feline Forum was not only touching but a true lesson in the rewards received by following one's instincts. Mia provided Catherine with the greatest gift a feline can offer their owner... that being their total trust. Mia began life as a caged feline trapped in a cattery operating as a kitten breeding mill. It can take many years for these fearful queens to learn that not all people will neglect or be cruel to them. Despite Mia's situation she quickly passed through the stages of bonding because Catherine's unique energy was in harmony with her own.

I believe Catherine needed Mia's presence in her life for quite a while. Although she had lost two beloved cats, she was still emotionally seeking the comfort of another feline; this was the energy she was projecting to the Universe long before the day she encountered Mia.

In Catherine's words, *"Yesterday after work I went out for a drive in the country with Maggie, my adopted Greyhound. However I got caught in traffic at the tunnel on my way back home. Rather than sit in line, I got off the main road and decided to follow the river hoping I would come across another route back."*

No one likes being stuck in traffic, however I prefer to believe that Catherine was following her destiny. She selected a road which lead to the right SPCA facility holding her beloved Mia. It has been my experience that only when the time is right will such a detailed path lead to a Feline Soul Mate. Had she made any other decision then Mia wouldn't have become such an important part of her life. Despite owning a large dog and faced with the decision of adopting a fearful cat, Catherine instinctively knew she was following the right path.

May we all have the same courage to continue on such a journey, especially when circumstances dictate that it may be easier to turn back. Perhaps it's better to listen to one's inner voice when interpreting complicated details concerning matters of the heart. For only when our instincts are in unison with our hearts will such a decision bare results that are as equally rich and rewarding.

*Loneliness is comforted by the closeness*
*and touch of fur to fur, skin to skin - or skin to fur.*
**- Paul Gallico**

# True Reflections
- by Sande Kay

*Women, poets, and especially artists, like cats; delicate natures only can realize their sensitive systems.*
- Helen M. Winslow

In 1978, while living in Rhode Island, I was introduced to what was then a rare and dying breed: Maine Coons. The female I met was so wonderful, friendly, *large* and personable I decided then and there that 'some day' one of those large wonderful cats was going to share my life. Well, my 'some day' did not come for another 20 years! I continued to learn all that I could about the breed and communicate with the original breeder during those long years. Twenty years later when I finally finished my youthful travel, I happened upon a Maine Coon breeder in my area. She had just had a litter of kittens (two!) and asked me if I was interested in visiting. She told me the kittens were not available, as she was going to keep both, but I could visit. And visit I did! Several times.

At about four weeks, the little male decided that I was a good substitution for his littermate. I did not know it at the time, but we were bonding; there was a magic between us, a spark. Luckily, the breeder was aware of this and she agreed that I could actually have this kitten! The day this breeder brought him to my house for his first 'visit' he curled up in my lap and purred. When it was time to go (it was only a visit), he dug his claws in and hung on to my jeans for dear life. Though he was only ten weeks old, she let me keep him then and there. She said, "He has made his choice."

And I did feel chosen! For the next ten years True (that was his name) sat with me, ate with me, slept on my papers when I was trying to work and hid my paintbrushes while I painted. He was the cat of my heart. When I experienced massive self doubt as I began to show my paintings professionally, he stayed near me in my studio every day while I painted. He actually posed for his own painting and wouldn't let me quit. He would vocalize if I didn't go into the studio to paint. I have photos of his furry self posing for his painting on my studio table. More than anyone else in those first years, he encouraged me to keep going, keep painting. I know it sounds odd, but you try to ignore a 25-pound cat who is wrapping himself around your ankles, gently herding you toward the studio. It is rather impossible. His quiet persistent presence while I painted was exactly what I needed to continue.

During the recent tainted pet food epidemic, he developed Liver Failure in response to tainted pet food he ate. We both fought our hardest. He was fed lovingly by tube every hour for almost *three months*. In the end, I had to let him go. He was so sick. True crawled up onto my lap and spent his last hours there. Just as he had entered my life, he exited in the same manner. I miss him still. We both tried, and even though I am supposed to be the one 'in charge,' in the end I could not save him. Letting him go was the toughest decision I ever made. I question myself every day about what I should have done differently. I miss all 25 pounds of him sitting on my lap. Although he never went to a cat show, he was the cat of my heart and my True Champion.

True in his garden 'helping' Sande write her dissertation

*May you leave this life knowing you were well loved;*
*May your steps away from me bring us closer in heart;*
*And May you walk, my friend,*
*Freely,*
*In Peace*

True (aka King True)
Born October 12, 1997 - Died April 20, 2007
You will always be my bunny-furred boy.

# Rusty and the Pilot
### - by Jasmine Kinnear

*People that don't like cats haven't met the right one yet.*
### - Deborah A. Edwards

In my first years of breeding I encountered several couples where the wife loved cats unconditionally while the husband merely tolerated them. Such was the case with the pilot and his wife.

During the placement of Tara's second litter of kittens I had the pleasure of meeting Beth. With grown children no longer at home Beth was experiencing 'empty nest syndrome'. After some pressuring, her husband had reluctantly consented to a kitten's presence in their home.

During her first visit to the cattery Beth stayed for over an hour watching Tara's kittens at play. She finally selected my favourite kitten, a little Red Tabby male who she would eventually name Rusty.

Rusty

When selling a kitten I would normally request a standard deposit to consider the baby sold. However Beth provided payment for her kitten in full. Without words being exchanged, I knew she felt more secure by fully purchasing her little male. Beth was determined that her husband would not have an opportunity to change his mind before her kitten's homecoming.

Prior to Beth leaving I advised her to come back as often as she was able to visit with her new kitten. She sighed and thanked me but confided that her husband didn't care for cats saying, "I'm sorry but we've been looking for a while and he's never even come in to see any of the kittens." Sure enough, I looked out the window to see Stephen sitting in the car passing the time by reading a book while he waited for his wife.

I explained to Beth that in my experience many men who proclaimed to dislike cats simply hadn't been introduced to the right one. I knew that she had selected a special kitten who was both adventurous and loving. He had inherited his mother's gentle nature and displayed many of his father's endearing idiosyncrasies. He was a sweet male and would become a contented lap cat making an ideal companion for their family, especially her reluctant husband. This Red Tabby Persian was also the perfect male kitten to bond with a man who had never loved a cat before.

"Your husband will love him," I reassured her and mentioned she would adore Rusty so much that she'd be back in the spring for another kitten. Despite the look of doubt on her face I further predicted it would be her husband who would be the one seeking a second cat. At the time she shook her head in disbelief, but long before spring she called again asking if I had any more kittens available.

It was Christmas time and Candace had a litter of six kittens ready for viewing. Beth confirmed that I had been right about her husband. In fact, Rusty had bonded so tightly with Stephen that she really needed a kitten for herself. Rusty loved her but he was attached and totally devoted to Stephen. Rusty always selected Stephen's lap and would sleep next to him at night when he was off duty and home in the evenings. She admitted there were times when she felt jealous, confessing she was uncertain if it was Rusty's or her husband's full attention that she was actually missing.

Stephen was a commercial pilot who spent long periods of time away from home. However when he was not working Rusty became his cat and never left his side. This time when Beth returned to the cattery Stephen came in with her, anxious to view the kittens.

As Beth and Stephen watched the kittens at play, Stephen spoke in glowing terms of how much he enjoyed his Rusty. As a breeder there's no experience sweeter than listening to a man speak with such affection for his cat. This was especially true for me as I'd nursed a quiet suspicion that Rusty would charm Stephen into becoming a cat lover.

Although the couple were selecting a new addition to their family for Beth, it was Stephen who decided he wanted Cricket, a sweet Blue Persian male. The couple stayed for several hours while Stephen recounted his favourite stories about life with "his boy," Rusty. I assured them that when their new kitten was mature and able to leave the cattery I would provide instructions on the best manner to introduce the two half brothers.

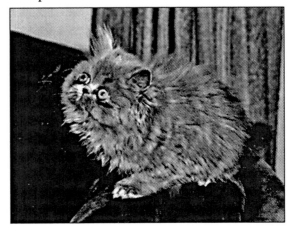

Cricket

The following spring Beth telephoned again hoping I had another litter of kittens available to view. This time however the kitten was intended for her engaged daughter visiting from the East Coast. Melissa loved Rusty and Cricket and had made the decision that she wanted one of my kittens as a wedding gift from her parents.

The engaged couple anxiously arrived at the cattery and selected a Blue Point Himalayan female they would eventually name Lucy. When the kitten was sixteen weeks old Stephen arrived dressed in his pilot's uniform to pick up Lucy. The baby was going to ride in the cockpit with her personal pilot; there would be no cargo hold for her. Stephen proudly told me he intended to deliver the kitten to his daughter in person. How wonderful it was to see a man who appreciated felines so much!

Within six months I received a telephone call from Melissa in Ontario. Lucy had settled in well, however they were anxious for her to have company. It was important to Melissa that the kitten be related to Lucy and she felt more comfortable purchasing her new baby from me. Melissa requested that it be my choice as she trusted I would select a kitten who would be compatible with Lucy's personality. A few months later Stephen arrived at my door once again to pick up a Seal Point Himalayan female who would be named Cookie. Cookie was also flown in the cockpit with her own personal pilot. I was later told that I couldn't have made a better choice as both girls became totally devoted to each other.

I respected Beth for always maintaining contact and consulting me whenever she had questions or problems with her cats. After selling four kittens within the same family Beth and I kept in touch long after I stopped breeding. She was one of my buyers who encouraged me to become a Cattery Consultant and writer to assist other buyers and novice breeders. Years after selecting Rusty she confided to me that I was not the first cattery she had visited. However she simply knew she was in the right place and made her selection based on the breeder and not just the kittens.

Beth and Stephen left a lasting impression and created wonderful memories of my cattery years. I can still recall the expression on Stephen's face whenever he came to select a new kitten. Such encounters last a lifetime for a breeder as placing the right kitten in the perfect home is a wonderful accomplishment. The last time Beth and I spoke she was pleased to inform me that Stephen was still a devoted cat lover. She was comforted knowing that she'd never be alone in her home without a feline ever again. For as all ailurophiles know there is a special magic in a cat's presence; a cat truly makes a house into a loving home.

*There are few things in life more heart warming*
*than to be welcomed by a cat.*
- Tay Hohoff

# The Condo Kitty of Rothwell Street
- by Jasmine Kinnear

*The city of cats and the city of men exist one inside the other,*
*but they are not the same city.*
**- Italo Calvino**

Vancouver Island is well known for its generosity and kindness towards pets in need. During the non-relenting winter storms this season I remembered another storm and a gentle tabby male who came to be known as the Condo Kitty of Rothwell Street.

The Esquimalt neighbours believed this sweet boy once lived in an old house on Bowlsby Street behind Rothwell. When his elderly owner died the house was sold and subsequently demolished. With the loss of his owner this gentle male became yet another homeless feral struggling to survive. His life however drastically changed on Christmas Eve of 1996 when the snowstorm of the century engulfed our island.

He appeared at the back door of a large Heritage house on Rothwell which had been converted into four condos. Each family tried to adopt him however he refused to stay indoors. Having lived as a feral cat for months it was his wish to remain outside enduring the worst snowstorm in living memory. Consequently it was decided everyone would share in the care of this little domestic male.

Beloved by all, each family contributed to the cost of the tabby's new residence. A carpenter was quickly hired to build a luxury outdoor two-level kitty condo. In his new home Chubby remained comfortably sheltered from the heat, rain and cold becoming a cherished and contented domestic.

Due to his stocky build his owners fondly named him

Chubby. As a newly adopted cat Chubby was naturally fearful and shy. Although he never strayed far from his benefactors in the beginning, he was reluctant to permit anyone to touch him. Gradually though he became familiar with his new name and more comfortable with the families caring for him. Eventually he positioned himself to greet everyone on their way to and from work. While the children from the condos played in the yard Chubby would remain nearby protecting the property from both strangers and migrating felines.

One family took charge of his dietary requirements serving him daily on clean dishes. This family was also diligent during the summer adding ice cubes to freshen his water and provided a warm comforter during the winter months. Another family paid for his vet care while still another provided freshly washed linen for his bed every day. His condo was placed in a protected area between two doors leading to separate suites. Chubby developed a loving bond with his new owners and would randomly scratch at a chosen family's door whenever he desired some inside warmth and company.

Early each morning Rothwell St.'s shy tabby would venture out to the front of the house to keep watch over the property. I first encountered this sweet male while assisting my son Mark deliver his flyers. After meeting the neighbours I was told of Chubby's high status as Rothwell St.'s Condo Kitty. Chubby initially considered me a stranger. Yet despite his shyness I eventually won his favour after many months of pampering and spoiling him with kitty treats. As we delivered flyers early in the morning I was the first person to greet Chubby on weekends. Our twice weekly encounters grew to include cuddles and of course the expected kitty treat I carried especially for him. Having experience with cats I assisted with his grooming and would also refresh his water before leaving. I was especially touched by the devotion of the families in providing such a loving home for a displaced cat.

I grew to love him during our encounters, calling him Cherub rather than Chubby. I believe in the theory that every name carries an energy that will eventually influence that feline's life. When accentuating the positives you actually draw positive energy into your cat's life. Therefore with a name like Chubby he was simply encouraged to overeat and become less active. Although several friends doubted this theory, given time they came to accept how their chosen name did accentuate unexpected traits in their felines. In Chubby's case he did indeed follow the energy dictated by his name by growing rounder and more content with each passing year.

I saw Chubby less often when Mark stopped delivering flyers. However whenever driving past his home I would visit his condo, bringing a small supply of nutritious treats. Although several weeks would often pass when Chubby was not home I still left treats by his condo. Even a year later Chubby still recognized me and I was given a warm greeting only reserved for the special people in his life.

At that time I was a registered cat breeder and had never shared intimate contact with outside felines. I hold near and dear the memories of those cats I befriended on our route developing a new perspective of the outside domestic. Over the years I have met others who have adopted stray cats however there was something about Chubby and his four families that touched me deeply. It was a wonderful experience and typical of Victoria to see a rescued stray adopted and living in contentment. Several years ago Chubby's condo disappeared from the back of the building. I've always hoped that in his senior years Chubby finally made his choice and selected one family to enjoy an indoor condo retirement.

Hopefully such generosity of spirit was extended to those pets who also found themselves lost during this year's winter storms. For those who have welcomed into their home a cat in need such as Chubby may your blessings be many. When you have been chosen by a cat you soon appreciate how special a bond that relationship will become. I also wish to extend my deepest respect and gratitude to those volunteers working diligently in the worst of weather to save other lost felines. In life you only keep what you give away, this especially being true in matters of the heart.

*The cat is the only animal which accepts the comforts*
*but rejects the bondage of domesticity.*
- **Georges Louis Leclerc de Buffon**

# Barney, The Green Pawed Moggie
## - by Pat Chalmers & Jasmine Kinnear

*When she walked... she stretched out long and thin like a little
tiger, and held her head high to look over the grass
as if she were treading the jungle.*
*- Sarah Orne Jewett*

In the life of a feline a series of events must come to pass
before a feral kitten may be transformed into a green pawed
moggie. Such is the story of Barney who became the beloved
feline of the Chalmers family in Corby, Northamptonshire,
England.

Barney was born in a litter of five black and white tuxedo coloured kittens. As the product of two feral moggies, his lineage was most likely generation upon generation of feral breeding. A kitten born under such circumstances is predestined to live a short and difficult life. However due to the kindness of the children of Corby this was not to be the fate for Barney or his four littermates.

A small group of young Corby children found a moggie queen lost and in need of care. Sensitive to her needs, rather than leaving her to cope on her own they knocked on one door after another hoping to find her a home. Upon reaching the home of Pat Chalmers she fondly recalls the children asking, *"This poor cat is a stray, can you take her in?"* Having never owned a cat before Pat was uncertain of the care necessary for the female. However, concerned over the queen's welfare she informed the children, *"I would love to, I'd better not though, I hope you find someone who does! Please come back and let me know."*

According to Pat the children's search eventually ended when they reached the home of her son's best mate known as Little James. Maureen, his Mum, answered the door and when the children told their story she replied, *"Yes, of course we'll look after her."*

The shy black and white queen had found a loving home and was given the name of Lucy. Maureen was soon to realize that Lucy had not arrived alone as she was carrying an unexpected gift for her new family. Just a little pregnant at the time, within six weeks she delivered a beautiful litter of five black and white moggie kittens. Although the blessed event was unexpected, the five additional kittens didn't appear to bother Maureen. However, in all kindness she decided eventually a trip to the veterinarian was in order for her female. These babies were to be Lucy's final litter once the kittens were weaned and living in their new homes.

As close mates, James Chalmers and Little James spent the

next month playing with Lucy's growing kittens. James seriously wanted one of Lucy's kittens, although the Chalmers family had never known the many blessings from owning a feline. He embarked on a campaign determined to convince his parents in the merits of adopting one of Lucy's moggie babies. According to Pat she finally relented and recalls, *"James kept saying how adorable they all were. I finally said yes because he kept on and on and on!"* Eventually Lucy and her entire litter were brought to the Chalmers' front parlour for a formal introduction.

The active litter was confined to the living room with Pat watching in amazement as the kittens proceeded to climb the curtains, scratch her furniture and genuinely make themselves at home. She experienced a few anxious moments regretting her decision. In her words, *"There they all were clambering up my curtains and climbing up polished wood antiques. I started seriously wondering what I had gotten myself into."*

One little male preferred to sit quietly on the fireplace hearth and only watched his littermates at play. With five active six-week-old kittens, it was a difficult choice for James to decide on the perfect kitten.

*"Which one do we pick Mum?"* James asked.

Despite Pat's inexperience with kittens, she felt herself drawn to the little one by the fireplace hearth quietly observing everyone in the living room.

*"I think this one,"* she said thoughtfully, referring to the same male who was silently observing his new environment. *"I believe he belongs here James."* She warmly recalled the scene from so many years before, *"...and there was Barn sitting next to me by the fireplace, like the good boy he was!"*

The entire Chalmers family soon grew to love the new feline addition to their home. However it was the kitten himself who selected Pat as his special person. Naming a cat is an important decision, and upon placing some careful thought Pat finally selected the name of Barney. During our interview for this book I was pleased to hear the story behind such a special name for a dignified kitten.

Having a long history with felines, I am convinced that a cat's name will play an important role in their destiny. My theory is every name carries with it an energy that will strongly influence that feline's life. When you accentuate the positives you actually draw positive energy into your kitten's life. Pat innocently tapped on to the Ying/Yang Universal energy of striking a balance between the passive feminine and the active masculine side of her moggie's nature. With an instinctive awareness supporting this belief, Pat chose the name of Barney, drawing from a special time that the family experienced each year.

For their holidays the Chalmers family enjoyed travelling to the County of Suffolk. It became a family tradition to stay at a small hotel known as Smith's Knoll located in Lowestoft. After many years they became regarded as a part of the family and were warmly welcomed by the proprietors, Barney and Dora Smith. Pat fondly remembers Barney as being quite a character. Although the couple have long since retired Pat fondly recalls, *"I can still hear his accent in my head. Barney was one of a kind hailing from the East of England, his accent was his alone. Barney Smith was so droll, so laid back, so different, he had expressions all of his own."*

Barney and Dora Smith

Barney would frequently entertain the Chalmers in his Suffolk accent with stories about his life as a fisherman at sea. Pat when choosing a name for her new kitten, tapped on to the love and kindness of Barney and his wife Dora. Barney the fisherman was delighted once informed of his namesake in the form of a moggie residing in the Chalmers' home in Corby.

The name was an ideal choice for a feral kitten adapting to a new home. As time passed, blessed with the warm name of Barney, this kind man's positive energy gently influenced the shy kitten.

I told Pat of the benefits from her choice of a name that represented a time of great happiness in her life. Positive energy would be reflected in her voice every time she called his name or was physically interacting with her kitten. Having a feral background Barney was shy with everyone, however he responded to Pat's love and tightly bonded with his new Mum.

*Prowling his own quiet backyard or asleep by the fire,*
*he is still only a whisker away from the wilds.*
**- Jean Burden**

Bonding and developing a relationship with a kitten will be a special experience for each family member. When I asked Pat about the length of time she needed to bond with her shy kitten she responded, *"That's easy! I loved Barn and knew he was something special from the very first day. However he did love clinging on to me with all fours at the ankles first thing in the morning, it sure woke me up."* While Barney was small this remained his personalized greeting every morning for his new Mum.

With such devotion from Pat, her male was provided with exactly the right care. Barney personifies the personality of the *Sophisticated Feral* which is taken from my *Felines by Design* series of books as excerpted below:

Loving patience is the key as this feline is slow to trust but gradually like a blossoming flower will mature responding to his owner's affections. They are a 'jewel in the rough' requiring a compassionate owner who is willing to permit these felines the luxury of time before bonding.

Despite Pat's inexperience with kittens she displayed an unusual degree of sensitivity with her moggie; she was truly an exception to the rule. She knew Barney required unconditional love and displayed great patience concerning his preference of care. Feral kittens are best suited for the experienced cat lover who is willing to accept these babies just as they are. Pat's sensitivity and respect of his timid nature permitted him the luxury of time to become comfortable with the loss of his mother and littermates. Providing such personalized care was ideally suited to Barney and he quickly blossomed within the loving environment of the Chalmers' home. As a result, Barney and Pat developed a tight emotional attachment and soon considered their relationship to be a lifetime commitment. The following excerpt is again taken from the *Sophisticated Feral* personality and is reflective of Pat and Barney's developing relationship:

> It has been my experience that with the right person these babies eventually learn to love and trust their owners. Like a long anticipated wait for a fine bottle of wine, these lovely cats are exceptional when they gradually become comfortable in their home. As the Sophisticated Feral matures they remain deeply attached to their owner in a manner unlike any other Feline by Design. With time and respect the results of the bonding, although a more prolonged and individual process are truly outstanding.

As the months passed Pat says, *"He developed a passion for some of my cooking and wouldn't leave you alone till he got some! Macaroni cheese with cheese sauce drizzled over the top, the gravy from braising steak, liver with kidney, a few slices of the Sunday joint are just but a few. He thrived and it didn't seem to do him harm, he was always a well boy even though he stayed on the lean side."*

74

Pat is a gifted gardener and is well known in her area for being expertly green fingered. One only has to see her garden to perceive the love and dedication she devotes to her plants. Barney soon became her green pawed assistant and they would spend hours tending their flower beds together. Over the years the Chalmers' garden developed into a virtual showplace of flowers and plants. Pat's vast gardening knowledge has earned her the status of a Master Gardener by many of her friends and neighbours. Known for her kindness, she donates many hours tending to the plants and gardens of friends and senior citizens in Northamptonshire.

As Pat shared her love of gardening with Barney it brought them great enjoyment together. She was hesitant to continue because she didn't believe anyone would believe her cat's ability as her gardening apprentice.

*"The way he used to scratch the soil in the garden every time I was using my trowel to dig a hole, after that it was a recognised thing between him and me. I used to say come on Barn, we've got some planting to do. When I would dig a hole with my trowel to plant something, Barn would move in scratching away, tossing the soil everywhere. I used to say to him be more tidy will you Barn, you know your Mum is a Virgo, it has to be neat.*

*It was ever so funny really, just like he was really trying to help me. One night at supper I started to tell the boys about it, they just looked at me sideways though as if to say how many has she had tonight?*

*It was just Barn's and my secret. Every time I was going to plant something, I'd say come on Barn, I need your scratching out, we have planting to do. Although the garden was his personal territory, when it came to the plants he was very careful. He'd never touch anything and would jump over everything. He never damaged a plant because he knew that he didn't have to. I simply told him to sniff and move saying, 'Barn this is precious.' He always came and helped me till his later years, and then I just used to leave him to sleep in the greenhouse.*

*Everyone always commented that Barney acted more like a dog than a cat. I know every cat is pleased to see his owner back home, however this is difficult to explain. Every time I appeared from wherever, and it didn't matter how far away he was, Barney would run like a wild rabbit to greet me because I was home. I don't know... perhaps all cats do that?"*

Pat and Barney, soul mates forever

Pat is not alone as many other cat lovers I have met are equally perplexed upon the appearance of a Feline Soul Mate in their lives. The new addition to their home is unlike any other feline they have ever encountered before. It soon becomes apparent to the mistress that their newly acquired cat is rather different. This perception is probably true because I find many of these special cats are simply unable to accept the status of being a feline. The cat emanates an unique energy and quickly acquires the most intimate understanding of their person. It is during this bonding process that the owner realizes the extent of the blessed gift they have been given in finding their feline. Many are perplexed with their cat's ability to anticipate every move they are going to make.

*In nine lifetimes, you'll never know as much about your cat as your cat knows about you.*
**- Michael Zullo**

I inform them that that the answer is simple, "This cat is your Feline Soul Mate and not entirely feline. You may find he will understand you on the same level as your closest friend and deepest confidant."

I may say this and yet I know, with time, their relationship will evolve well past such comparisons. By using such intimate relationships as an example, the perplexed owner is then able to appreciate their feline's distinctive qualities. It is only with the passing of time as their relationship matures, will the magnitude of their feline's blessings within their life become truly apparent. How could I ever prepare an owner for the experience awaiting them when sharing their lives with such a precious cat? The exchange often will occur during the intimate vibration of a purr. Then slowly it becomes apparent that the feline's heart is truly focused to meet their person's deepest emotional needs. There is an intimacy in the physical exchange of your feline's heartbeat against your own while he is resting on you. It is often in those moments that it is finally understood how deeply personal a relationship with a Feline Soul Mate can be.

In listening to the love reflected in Pat's voice I understood that she had truly found her own Feline Soul Mate. I then shared with her some of the material I was preparing for my book *The Feline Soul Mate Mystique*. However it was Pat's sensitive nature and loving respect for all things living that truly touched me. She was looking forward with great anticipation to a large garden show and I mentioned I shared the same feelings when attending a cat show.

*"Cat shows must be just so fascinating, I wonder to myself if the general public are allowed to stroke those beauties? I have never been to a cat show in my entire life, flower shows galore, cat shows never. You're not allowed to touch the plants, even though I have before now and have been told by a so-called professional to please look only! That was at Chelsea one year and me being me I said to the bloke, 'Oh I'm terribly sorry, but just look how beautiful that leaf variegation is, it was just crying out to be touched and fondled, I treat them all like my babies.' I promise you, in the end he was laughing instead of being real stern as he seemed to be before."*

Only someone as sensitive as Pat could have brought out the special qualities within her moggie. She regaled me with wonderful stories of her precious Barn. One of my favourites involved her new kitchen floor and demonstrated the love everyone in the Chalmers' family shared with their sweet boy.

*There is no more intrepid explorer than a kitten.*
*He makes perilous voyages into cellar and attic, he scales the roofs*
*of neighboring houses, he thrusts his little inquiring nose into*
*half-shut doors... he gets himself into every kind of trouble, and*
*he's always sorry when it is too late.*
**- Jules Champfleury**

*"Our beloved Barney the kitten was just under a year old, he*

*was a nervous boy, would always hide away from anything and everything. Things like the dust men emptying the bins, so much noise, he would run for his life! Kids trying to get at him because he was such a pretty boy. Motor bikes passing on the main road, anything noisy. Funny thing though right up until he was about two years old, every time the door bell went whether he was asleep or awake he'd just charge there like a puppy dog. If the people at the door should come in, well he wanted his privacy and then he'd just hide away again.*

*So it began with getting new vinyl put on the kitchen floor. First though, the wooden floorboards had to be repaired or else any faults would definitely stick out like a sore thumb under that fine stuff. Well that's all we could afford going back then.*

*It was summer and very hot. My husband Fred decided he was going to repair the floorboards himself. I wasn't looking forward to the mess but I knew he'd get there eventually. We ripped the old stuff off then realized there were more cracked floorboards than we originally thought. In England anyway under the floorboards it looks quite a minefield. Fred continued all day getting the old ones out and then replacing them by new ones.*

*We thought Barney was sleeping in his favourite place in the living room. After many long hours, Fred had mended all the floorboards and it was finally back in one piece again. But then I panicked! I checked the living room only to discover that my Barn was missing. At that time he was just a baby as well. We searched everywhere and couldn't find him in any room of the house. I finally confessed my worst fear to my husband. 'He's under the floorboards, he has to be, he likes dark places away from the world! I'm certain that's where he is. You'll have to get them all up again and rescue him right now because he's going to die under there.'*

*My Fred being the wonderful man he is did just that. He got every single floorboard up again while James and I just stood there crying and shouting for Barney! Fred went underneath the surface of the floor trying to find him, he simply had to be there. James and I searched everywhere else in the house while Fred stayed under the floor still looking for Barn.*

*After coming up from the floorboards Fred was exhausted but he wouldn't rest; he insisted on finding our boy. He finally left the house and went looking down the park for him. There was Barn down at the park sitting with at least six other moggies playing. Once he spotted Fred he ran following him home jumping all the hedges and walls as he went. I then cuddled Barney while Fred went back to work replacing the floorboards yet once again. I just marvelled at what a man will do for the love of a cat."*

Pat believes that Fred was as devoted to Barney as she was, despite the fact that he never openly confessed his affection for their boy. In Pat's words, *"I think that Fred bonded with Barn as quickly as I did although he wouldn't admit to such a thing. If I ever asked him such a question, he would just look at me sideways and ask, 'I don't know, do I?' I could just tell with his actions though and the things he used to say to our son. Sweet little things like 'Watch him James when he's washing, it's educational you know.' Fred was the one as well to be so meticulous about Barn's health making sure he always had his yearly flu jabs, flea jabs, etc, etc.*

*Fred also knew how much Barn loved the gravy from braising steak with all the fragments of meat in it. Due to his work hours, Fred had his dinner later than me and he used to warm it up himself. Of course there would be Barn smelling it and jumping up to taste a sample. Fred seemed to love that and always gave him a saucer full. Just the same thing happened when we were having Macaroni Cheese with homemade cheese sauce of course. Barn has such a passion for it and it seemed to give Fred a lot of pleasure as well. It became a nightly ritual because Barn wasn't going away until he got some of Fred's dinner."*

A young boy and a male kitten make ideal playmates and James and Barn were no exception. It was obvious how much Barney adored James, especially when they partook in games only the two of them appreciated. James would adorn him in assorted hats which Barney would proudly wear while they played. Although it amazed Pat, she claimed that one of their favourite games was for Barn to climb into the arms of sweaters where he'd stay purring his contentment. The two boys were great mates with James enjoying their cat as much as his mother did. She well understood that boys will be boys and would say, *"James, stop it will you, do you love him or what? Only thing was, Barney adored it, he always purred his head off when James was playing with him. The two of them made quite a pair."*

James and Barney

As caretaker of his Mum's beloved garden, Barney preferred to be outside. However he was also popular with the neighbours. Pat recalls another story when Barney displayed his unique charm throughout the neighbourhood.

*"Irene used to have a dog named Sooty from a pet rescue place. He was such a nervous boy and used to be literally frightened of anything that moved. If he should spot other dogs or cats he didn't bark, he just literally trembled.*

*Although Barney was a nervous cat, even in the beginning he loved to make his rounds throughout the neighbourhood. He enjoyed teasing the dogs while they were on their leads and took particular delight with teasing Shug while he was being walked by my dear friend Fiona."*

**A cat will sit washing his face within
two inches of a dog in the most frantic state of
barking rage, if the dog be chained.
- Carl Van Vechten**

*"Every morning Barney would be missing for the day. When he finally arrived home I would ask him, 'Where have you been? I was worried about you.' Barn however kept his secrets and would never let on about his adventures. However one day the cat was finally out of the bag when Irene and I had a visit.*

*She asked me, 'Did you know your Barn comes to my house every day and eats all Sooty's food?'*

*I said, 'Oh I'm ever so sorry.'*

*She replied, 'I'm not, he's the best thing that could have happened to Sooty. He's not frightened with Barney. Barney eats all his food then they snuggle down together and sleep for the day, sometimes they even cuddle each other.'"*

To know Pat is to love her; she gives from the heart to everyone so it didn't surprise me that Barney was the same. He kept migrating moggies out of his own garden as he knew his mother's plants were never to be used... even for his own purposes. Pat recalls several incidents when family members from Canada would arrive. Barn was displeased with the changes in his family's routine and especially with not having his Mum's full attention.

*"He was so jealous though if anyone should come to stay and he knew exactly how to get my attention. I was busy telling them he never sleeps on my borders. My Auntie Grace said, 'Well he is now.' There he was stretched right out in the middle of a flowering plant, heather actually. It was squashed to pieces and he knew I'd belt out there once I spotted him. He was very particular about the family members that visited.*

82

*Barney usually only cuddled with me as he wasn't the cuddly sort of moggie, however he also loved being held by my son's Gran. Although James' Gran wasn't exactly a cat lover either, with Barn she made the exception and he equally made the exception for her.*

*My Dad just adored cats, dogs, anything, with Barney being particularly special to him as well. Every time Mum and Dad were over here, my Dad would rub his fingers in front of him, wanting Barn to scramble up onto his lap. It all depended on Barney's mood of the moment though. Barn was inclined to be a bit on the snooty side sometimes, especially when anyone was here, even my own parents! It was like he used to think, 'Oh no, who's that sitting in my chair, hope you're not going to be stopping overnight, what will I do then?'*

*When we were home alone though, he used to put up a battle with Fred and James to get his favourite arm chair. If anyone else was here, well he was a scaredy cat. He just suffered in silence if you like, running to me whimpering like a scalded child to make his world right again."*

Barney,
King of his domain

However the day did arrive when Pat decided perhaps it would be nice for Barn to have his own feline company. Pat was enjoying her boy so much she decided a female would be perfect for him.

*"Then there was that so pretty stray cat that wandered into my garden, she was just adorable. Barney was livid I had taken another cat in. I still think of her now. She was so pretty, so affectionate, so pregnant!!! She used to scramble in the car with Fred and perch on his shoulders when he went to the paper shop. I think he quite liked it really, pity another one like her isn't passing my way.*

*I finally decided that Barn was just too unhappy and although I loved her so much it was better to find her a new home. Fred simply mentioned it one day at work and within a few days there was a couple interested in her. One Monday night a man in a tuxedo and a lady in evening dress came to see if they would like to have her. I was praying they wouldn't want her when all the time I knew they wouldn't be able to resist her. When they came in to meet my girl she jumped off the kitchen chair. She stretched herself like they do and I immediately knew I'd lost her, she was looking far too pretty for my liking. Of course they wanted her immediately and took her right away. That was it, she was gone. While I sat and cried, Barney rejoiced because she was gone forever. Having another moggie for him all started because I thought the company would be good for him when we were on our holidays.*

*I remember going back to his younger days, we always had to put him in a cattery every time we went on holiday or down to Mum and Dad's for Christmas. I hated that but there was no choice and he hated it too. He seemed to pine as he always lost loads of weight while we were gone. He just didn't eat the same, wondering what he had done wrong I suppose.*

*On the day we arrived home I could never wait to go and collect him again. One year we arrived back about 7 pm. I just wanted my Barn home too but knew the cattery would be shut by then. Even so I persuaded my husband to drive out there just to make sure it was definitely closed. Well I suppose someone had to be there really with all those cats to look after but I presumed they wouldn't be open to the public.*

*It was a place in the sticks, in other words deep in the country side. As we approached I spotted someone in the reception place working. I was so excited! It was a man working there and I explained we wanted our Barney even though I knew they were closed.*

*He said, 'I'm sorry my dear, I wouldn't have a clue where Barney is. I don't know where any of the cats are I'm just holding the fort till whoever returns.'*

*It was a big cattery, well I think it was big as it must have housed about 200 cats. I said to the bloke, 'I'll find him, I'll shout him and he'll come running!'*

*The bloke said, 'He won't will he? That might take you a fair old while there's a lot of cats here you know.'*

*I said, 'So if I find him and we pay the bill, we can take him, yes?' The bloke replied, 'Well I don't see why not, bet you won't find him though.'*

*It was a well laid out place, all the runs where the cats lived seemed to go on for miles. I went up and down the first four, screeching as loud as I could, 'Barney, where are you?' I have been blessed with a loud strong voice and perfect hearing. All of a sudden I knew I could hear him. He was a fair way up, I even missed out several aisles as I knew roughly where his voice was coming from. I ran with the bloke plodding on behind me and made the correct decision turning down the right aisle because suddenly there was my Barn. He was clawing up the wire looking really delighted because he knew he was coming home. As always he looked his usual bag of bones while staying at one of those places. However he soon made up for it when he got home by devouring about three dishes of food straight off."*

Pat apologized saying, *"I suppose this is typical of any cat owner and wouldn't make book material?"* I told her she was quite wrong and shared my personal experience with boarding my own two cats in Canada. I have also written an article on boarding cats during vacations for a magazine and understood exactly how she felt.

She confessed, *"It's just that it's one of the memories of Barn's dreaded cattery days. Not long after that though, it was catteries no more as he was such a lover of the garden. If we went away he preferred to live out there and would sleep in his precious greenhouse. Irene and Sooty would come round and gave him his food. I was so relieved because it always worked so well and ended Barn's cattery days once and for all, thank-goodness."*

Barney in the greenhouse keeping an eye on his cat grass

Loving a Feline Soul Mate requires little effort and will be second nature for many women. Its importance can be compared to that special time in life following the birth of your first child. The validity of the old wives tale passed down through the ages suddenly makes sense. Every parent will see their child as being the most beautiful baby in the nursery. I had heard this statement repeated by my father often as a child. Yet this became a personal and rather shocking reality for me following my only son's birth. The spiritual connection to my father with those same words repeated throughout my childhood by him resonated through me. It was true because I did have the most beautiful baby in the hospital. The awareness of this realization overwhelmed me and connected me to my father who died only two days following Mark's birth. It still remains a personal heartbreak that my father never held his only grandchild.

When I shared this confidence with Pat she agreed with my perception because as a mother with an only son she felt the same way. Loving Barney was second nature to her and the pride reflecting in her voice as she described his appearance was touching.

*"Tuxedo moggies may be quite common in the United Kingdom, however my sweet boy, well I've never seen another with markings as perfect as Barn's are! I know it doesn't matter a toss, but our Barn is some handsome boy. His markings are so perfect with each foot looking like he has socks on. The white bit on his chest is so perfect as well, looks like the top of a shirt under a tuxedo with the rest of him being a shining jet black. He always seemed like a long cat, not big, far from fat but perfectly made if you know what I mean."*

I knew exactly what she meant because my Tia has her own domestic beauty in both colouring and coat. Although she was born a feral moggie just like Barn there are days when her beauty outshines both my Persian male, Tally Ho and his Himalayan sister, Jewel. As a breeder I may have produced these felines myself however I still marvel at the incredible and natural beauty of a domestic feline.

The Chalmers' home was the perfect environment to draw out the very best in Barney's nature. He may have been adopted as a timid moggie, however he was greatly influenced by Pat's loving personality. When a cat is introduced to a child in an appropriate manner the resulting relationship can be quite special. Barney as a six-week-old kitten was introduced to James when he was only eleven and as a result they had the benefit of maturing together. Once James became a man their relationship naturally became a mutual camaraderie of two mates. Barney's kitten days were now behind him with the high activity level of children living within his home long forgotten.

Pat's dear friend Fiona was eventually blessed with a

daughter and as she matured Hollie developed a fascination for Barney. I had also loved cats my entire childhood but seldom had an opportunity to enjoy them. Hollie felt the same attraction and even at two years old was particularly drawn to Barney's gentle disposition.

*"When Hollie was small I would tell her that Barn wears his white fur socks to keep his feet warm. This only encouraged her interest with a growing desperation to have him like her. It may have been love at first sight for Hollie, Barney however took his time responding to the sweet little girl.*

*Every time when Hollie set her eyes on Barn she just wanted to get near him. She would charge all round my garden after him but never caught him as he always out ran her. After that, with the least sound of Hollie's voice, Barn ran a mile and hid until she was gone. Then I told her, 'He's a bit of a scared boy so be quiet towards him. You know whisper to him, don't run straight at him, you watch he'll love you for that.'*

*She was just dying to stroke him and for him to be her friend. She even would ask me if she could give him her crisps, chocolate or grapes. I would always tell her, 'Better not Hollie, it will give him a tummy ache.'*

*Time went by, Hollie was growing into a real little girl and so beautiful, well she's always been that. Each time she came here with her Mum, she would always ask, 'Where is Barney, I want to stroke him?'*

*Following her sixth birthday she came with Fiona for a visit. I knew Barn was curled up sleeping in the living room. She wanted to go to him however I told her, 'Remember what I said, you tiptoe through cause he's fast asleep. You just stroke him gently, he'll purr, I promise you.'*

*She did that and to her sheer delight he did purr. This time just as I promised he didn't run away from her. He then walked through to the kitchen and I said to Hollie, 'Would you mind giving Barn his dinner?'*

*She spooned it into his dish, the floor too, but that was fine because she was just so in her element. Barn ate what she served him and she watched him like she hadn't seen anything or anyone eat before. Then he looked up and said miaw looking up at her. I told Hollie, 'He's thanking you for his dinner, now he wants out.' So she opened the door and let him out into his garden. The best part was seeing how pleased she was with herself.*

*Hollie was equally thrilled by Barney's nocturnal visits to see her. He would travel to her home walking through the snow leaving his footprints all over the back garden. She remembers sitting on her father's lap waiting to see Barney press his nose against the window as a personal greeting. Barney didn't want to come into the house, he just wanted Hollie to see him and would leave once his presence had been acknowledged.*

*It just seemed better and better after that with Hollie and Barn. He didn't run away from her ever again and always let her stroke him. As they became closer she was overjoyed when he'd let her fuss over him and feed him and do anything she wanted with him. Hollie became a devoted cat lover with Barn being equally charmed by her. Also every Christmas and on his birthday she would always buy him a pressie, special cat treats to eat or a favourite toy. I know her Mum and Dad had something to do with it, even so, she loved Barn with all her heart."*

**Who would believe such pleasure from a wee ball o' fur?**
**- Irish Saying**

*"Barney was always a little rascal for being attracted to cars and used to love snoozing right underneath them. I always worried about him insisting on being outside every night but there was no way of changing his habits. I finally accepted that my Barn was just an outdoor boy at heart. I do believe though that somehow he must have been blessed with more than his nine lives. He was often in fights coming home with skin*

somewhere or other hanging off. I never knew what mischief he'd get himself into next. He loved the underneath of cars but hated being inside them, of course this made trips to the vet a challenge. He really used to let you know he hated travelling in our car. He'd never shut up until he was on the vet's table, and then he would just purr and be putty in her hands.

The vets always spoiled him and he so loved all the attention. Well there was that one exception, a vet Barney sensed I wasn't that struck on either. He was rather an unpleasant man and instinctively I knew he wasn't a nice person at all. Barney apparently felt the same way and didn't care for him either. He let the vet know our impression of his abrupt bedside manner and bit him hard enough to draw blood. In the future it was mutually agreed that Barn would only be examined by his select vets of preference.

Ever since he was a baby, with his habit of snoozing underneath the cars, I never really stopped worrying about him. He arrived home one morning in great agony with half his skin hanging off right to the bone. It was pretty obvious it must have been a car that hit him. I'll never know for sure with it being such a stormy night that anything might have happened.

Our vet said it was a fractured pelvis and that he must be kept indoors. We were told that he'd never run or jump properly again and may be quite an invalid. I nursed Barn for weeks but it was the keeping him indoors that was the problem. He was dopey when we brought him home, but regardless he still wobbled to the door and insisted on going out. For weeks on end I had to go out with him while he sniffed and worked his way round the garden. Barn never looked back after he recovered and still took delight in teasing the neighbourhood dogs and protecting his garden.

Being such an outdoor boy also included being in charge of every living thing in his garden. So many mornings when I first opened my kitchen door, there was a bird of some sort *lying there. Blackbirds, sparrows, thrush, even a big fat pigeon once. My immediate reaction was to feel cross with him. I used to say, 'Oh Barn, what have you done? That bird had a right to live its life too, now you've killed it.' He just looked at me and miawed as much as to say, 'Don't you think I'm a clever boy then?' Well of course he was a clever boy, it's a cat's nature to do that so how could I be cross with him?*

*One time there was such a commotion out in the garden, sparrows were dive bombing and squawking all over the place, everyone came out to see what on earth was going on! It was just our Barn toying with a frog and protecting his garden. That was until the frog jumped on his back and he ran for his life, completely going off that idea; birds were easier and far more predictable."*

**Okay, cats will never bring you pictures they've drawn in school,**
**but they may give you a dead mouse.**
**What parent could resist that gift?**
**- Terri L. Haney**

*"As the years passed I didn't want to accept the changes in Barney. He was still my green pawed gardening moggie and held such a place in my heart. I remember someone referring to him as an old boy and I became quite angry. I truly felt tempted to evict them right from my home for such an insult."*

I mentioned to Pat that despite my experience with felines I also had great difficulty accepting the fact that my own cats were aging. Barney's gardening years became a loving chronicle for the family and after seventeen years of protecting his home Barney's narrative was highly regarded in Corby. It was during this period while interviewing Pat that the events in Barney's story became especially touching. He was born a timid feral moggie and was not only loved by his own family but also worked his magic within the lives of others. When a feline is loved as Barney was, the mischievous side of his personality overcame his timid nature. His tendency to tease dogs as they were being walked and his ability to lovingly manipulate his Mum into providing his favourite dinners only further endeared him to Pat. She didn't want to accept his new status as a mature moggie as he still enjoyed entertaining her, much as he had as a kitten. Barney appeared ageless to those who loved him even when Pat realized that he had out lived every one of his littermates.

While I was compiling my notes for Barney's story I received an e-mail from Pat regarding her beloved boy. That long weekend proved to be a difficult time for both of us; we therefore kept in contact, for Barn's story was nearing an end. With Pat's permission I have provided her correspondence as only she could relay the intimate details she experienced with her sweet green pawed boy.

*"On November 18th, 2006, around 10 a.m., I heard a loud crying sound. It came from the garden and I rushed out to see what it was. All I could see was Barney sitting round the side just staring at the ground. Immediately I knew something was terribly wrong. I talked to him but he was quiet and didn't answer me as he always had. He just looked up from the ground not making any sound at all. He tried to walk but apparently something was wrong with his back legs as he was dragging them behind him. I lifted him up and rushed in the house saying to Fred, 'Quickly, we have to take Barn to the vet, something is seriously wrong, I just know it is.'*

*We got him into his cat carrier which normally he detested, however this time it was no effort at all. When he's in the car going to the vet he usually never stops speaking to me. He's always been a very insistent boy and quite demanding when it comes to his horrible cat carrier. This time though, silence, not one flicker of a miaw. That poor boy must have suffered not being able to make himself heard, he was normally such a chatterbox. It really bothered me terribly that he had lost his voice and couldn't make himself heard. With my heart pounding I was so worried about what the vet's verdict would be. I suppose really I already knew very well myself.*

*When we arrived at the vet we waited for what seemed an eternity for our turn. I'm thankful to say it was an experienced vet on that day, so caring and such a beautiful person. Barney always loved being on the vet's table in the past, no matter if he was getting flu jabs, flea jabs or anything. He just seemed to love the fuss and attention and they always spoiled him because he was such a handsome boy. He would just sit there with a deafening, non-stop purr. This time however, he was so silent.*

*After I had explained Barney's episode in the garden the vet gently examined him. Well she was such a good listener and I was so grateful for her compassion. Then she announced, 'Well he's an old man now, such a beautiful boy though.' She fondled him so lovingly and then she calmly said, 'I could take a load of tests, I could let you pay ridiculous amounts of money but what point is there? I'll give him a steroid injection and hopefully that will settle him a bit. If not please bring him back on Monday and we can speak then of the kindest thing to do.'*

*That was it then. I knew it myself really but I just wanted to be so terribly wrong. We brought Barn back home and I placed him in the living room. His favourite place in the house and the first room he'd ever been in as a kitten seventeen years before. He limped over to the other end of the room and for the next two days, he hid behind our TV and stereo unit. The only time he came out was to drink a gallon of water. He didn't want out to sit in his favourite garden, he hardly ate and only drank and drank and drank.*

*Sunday arrived, still Barn was in his hidey hole behind the TV and stereo unit. More or less he remained quiet until the evening. Then he surprised us all by walking right across the living room. He just looked up at me as by now I knew he had lost his miaw. However as always he knew his Mum would understand whatever he needed. Finally he wanted outside so we went together as we always had throughout the years. He wandered to the front garden; I was amazed because even his limp seemed to have improved. He did what he had to, which I have to say thrilled me so much as he hadn't moved for over 36 hours. I picked him up to bring him back in the house, feeling a wee bit happier as he had actually wanted out in his beloved garden.*

*In the kitchen, he was once again horrendously sick and I realized how difficult the rest of the day was going to be. James and Fred came rushing to my aid with James talking to Barn, believing this was the end because we all thought enough is enough. However it wasn't the end for Barney. He got up and walked back into the living room to the security of his hidey hole. So then we spoke together as a family for as much as it was hurting, we had to do the right thing for Barn.*

*We decided to take him back to the vet's on Monday and managed to live through that terribly difficult weekend. Monday arrived and I felt all churned up which of course is normal considering how hard the day was going to be for us all. I checked on Barn and he was still in his same place in the living room where he could peacefully hear the sounds of his home. Five minutes later though he walked into the kitchen looking for me as he was hungry and wanted to eat. He even wound himself round my legs as he'd always done in the past. I gave Barney dinner and he ate the lot. He then wanted to go outside as had always been his way over the years.*

*I wasn't believing all this, I went with him as he wasn't safe on his own any more. He even looked a lot friskier than he had been the day before. I wasn't thinking things like the calm before the storm, I was just thinking, 'Oh thank God, my Barn seems to be getting better.' Even though he had definitely lost his miaw I thought we'll get by and I'll take care of him. I'll see no harm comes to him as long as he feels alright.*

*I confided all of this to my husband, and Fred could see Barn's improvement for himself. He said, 'We can't possibly*

*do this thing now, we could never live with our conscience.'*
*Fred is dead sensible over things and because he had*
*confirmed my feelings I felt myself lifted. However on Monday*
*evening unfortunately Barn's condition became worse. It was*
*obvious that our poor boy didn't know where he was. So much*
*so that James and I sat up the whole night with him. I didn't*
*sleep at all that night even though I'm known to be a nodder as*
*soon as I sit down in the evening.*

*The next day arrived and my James and I saw the sunrise*
*together. It was November 21st, 2006, and we knew it would be*
*the last day with our Barney. It was just a horrible daunting*
*thought. James was going to come too but he was so distressed,*
*I told him, 'No don't, remember Barn in the good days and*
*remember last night because what would I have done without*
*you?'*

*I held Barn, I was trembling and my heart was pounding but*
*I thought, 'At least soon you will be at peace. Even though*
*we're all going to miss you so badly, especially me. I know*
*that my life will never be the same without you.'*

*Fred and I came home with Barn's body as he belonged in*
*his beloved garden. However the both of us were emotionally*
*exhausted and felt a bit like zombies. We had been at the vet's*
*for well over an hour. When we arrived back, James was still*
*heartbroken. He asked, 'How did it go, was the vet nice to*
*him?' I told my son, 'She was just lovely, couldn't have been*
*kinder to him. She told us we were doing the right thing, he*
*was an old man who'd lived a wonderful life and that's what*
*counts.'*

*Then we had to bury him in the same garden that Barney and*
*I had created together. I couldn't stop crying while Fred dug*
*the hole. The postman even arrived at that point. I know him*
*well and he asked, 'Are you ok?' Through my tears, I replied,*
*'No, we're burying our Barn.' He replied, 'I'm so sorry, I'll*
*go now but you're strong and you'll get there.' Then Fiona*
*came to the house and we both just cried all day, talking about*

*Barn, and remembering how he used to tease Shug when he was on a lead. How Hollie used to run like a greyhound to try and catch him and how close they eventually became.*

*One thing that has dawned on me as I write this to you... Barn purred when I held him right at the end... just before that awful moment when the vet eventually found his vein. I hadn't realized he was still able to purr. So I have to believe he was thanking me for being there with him and that he knew just how much I loved him."*

Pat and I were in contact for several months following her loss. I had grown quite fond of Barney during the time we exchanged our cat stories. When you've experienced so great a loss such as a cat you've owned since your child was small, you need someone who understands how deeply you are grieving. Pat said she missed him the most in the evenings when it was his place to be lying on her lap. I told her how sincerely I understood her feelings. My male Tally Ho takes his place on my chest every evening in preparation for his daily grooming. He will patiently wait for me to lie in bed before making himself comfortable for the night.

For a long time I would cuddle Tally and think of Pat missing her Barn. My Tally is also aging and matured with my child as his devoted playmate. Tally remains my special boy in much the same way Pat adored her moggie. My eldest female is 15 years old now and will mother everyone, yet still plays like a kitten. Her place is on my lap while Tally rests his head under my chin and next to my heart. After receiving Pat's e-mail regarding her loss, I held Tally and wept tears of gratitude for his presence in my life. I deeply respected how much Pat missed this special time of day with her Barney most of all.

Slowly as word spread of the Chalmers' loss, they were told how important Barney had been to other families in Corby. I believe a cat has been special when others will also shed tears once hearing of his passing. *"Hollie has such a beautiful heart for one so young and she mourned Barney as well. She so wanted to put flowers on his grave and she did, beautiful yellow roses."*

Never having owned or lost a cat before, Pat needed to maintain contact with me regarding the emotions she was experiencing. It became important for her to mark his grave so that he wouldn't ever be forgotten. I told her that for as long as she lived he would stay close to her and in spirit would remain by her side as she gardened. Barney's spirit would continue to move in scratching away and tossing the soil especially within her heart and memories.

Pat remarked that it was so strange for me to respond as I did because her garden was really a sacred place for her.

*"I do feel closer to God when in the garden. I find it so stimulating... so everyone I ever lost in my life who meant something to me, when in the garden, they are with me too! I don't expect many others to understand but it's so true though. When I am alone in the garden this is the time that they speak to my heart. It is my belief that during these moments they are truly with me.*

*I was tidying the front garden up this afternoon, after yet another shower. I was making sure Barn's grave was neat and tidy. I really went into a world of my own though, staring at the space where he is buried and thinking so deeply of how things used to be. Although it has been more than six months, his memory still brings tears to my eyes. As you can probably tell from this e-mail, I miss him so badly, especially today for some reason.*

*Maybe now because it's the summer months and he wouldn't be far away from me in the garden or in the greenhouse; but now he's not there. It's just seems so strange without him this year. I gaze at his favourite snoozing places in the garden and that also brings tears to my eyes, I just can't help it.*

*So then it made me think of my Mum and the day she nursed him in her arms the whole day when he wasn't too well. I could hear her very words on that day. She had never been that struck on cats either but somehow with our Barn she felt differently. I know I've said this before, but it's true, when in the garden I am closer to God and to everyone I have lost and loved. I'd like to think that Barn is with the both of them now, sitting in Dad's lap and being cuddled in my Mum's arms. That thought brings me some comfort you know and that's how I like to remember my boy as I tend his garden."*

***When you're used to hearing purring and suddenly it's gone, it's hard to silence the blaring sound of sadness.***
***- Missy Altijd***

# The Gift from Diabetes
## - by Jasmine Kinnear

*Most of us rather like our cats to have a streak of wickedness.*
*I should not feel quite easy in the company of any cat that walked*
*about the house with a saintly expression.*
### - Beverly Nichols

Even as a small child I wanted one, a cat, but not just any coloured feline... I wanted a calico. I've been told in life to be careful what you ask for because it just might happen... and so my story begins. I didn't experience the uniqueness of a calico until my late thirties and now I couldn't picture my life without including the quirkiness of such a special feline.

A family friend living in my birth place of Montreal, Quebec contacted me with an urgent situation. After becoming ill with diabetes, Thelma asked if she could move into my home for the short remainder of her life. She knew of my love for cats and couldn't bring herself to part with her two domestic calicos. Finally my childhood desire to have a calico had been answered. I've always been too impulsive by nature. Therefore with naïve sincerity I embraced what would become a difficult yet endearing challenge. My friend then shipped her two cats 3,000 miles across the country to stay in my care while she sold her home. Although Thelma had family in Quebec, she knew her girls would be destroyed if their eventual welfare was to be decided by either of her sons.

Thelma had received the calicos from her vet when they were six months old. By that time their prior owner had declawed them however the girls had not been altered. Thelma had previously owned dogs and had recently lost her beloved poodle Boujeaux. In her senior years and with the onset of diabetes, she had wisely decided against owning another dog knowing it would prove too difficult to manage. She mentioned to her vet that if any cat ever needed a home to please contact her. Several months later he telephoned to inquire if she would accept two young sisters from the same domestic litter. She agreed and sight unseen instructed her vet to immediately alter them; the calicos girls had found a new home.

I had three cats of my own at the time: Tally Ho, my Persian male, Caterina, my Himalayan and a domestic female we'd named Tia. Living with my active son Mark, his budgie Perky and our three sweet cats I was provided with unique challenges on a daily basis. However despite the added responsibility I also looked forward to Thelma's adult company. Her two calicos, aged three years arrived in October. The two feline families then merged complete with hisses and spits followed by a mutual truce of reluctant acceptance. The girls eventually adjusted to their active new environment and even welcomed contact with my young son. In the beginning both girls were distant towards me and therefore I worked harder to gain their trust and affection. My work was cut out for me as from their perspective I was the one who had temporarily removed them from Thelma whom they both adored.

Misty and Christy were large cats, quite overweight from being fed a low nutrition and high fat diet. Once they were prescribed a balanced diet from my vet and started enjoying the benefits from increased play activity, both girls began slimming down. Although they continued to exhibit unusually high levels of stress, this too lessened as they adjusted to their new home.

Misty (left) being groomed by Christy

Misty was a slightly whiter calico and was so named by Thelma due to her misty coloured appearance. She had her sweet loving moments and at times was affectionate. However she would also display personality traits typical of cats suffering from low self esteem. It was my belief that Misty harboured a feline abandonment disorder which became more pronounced the longer I owned her. During Misty's more difficult moments she made her life miserable by demanding the exhausting role of Head Cat. This she accomplished by displaying the nastier side of her personality whenever her defensive nature shifted into a feline control mode. Although an intelligent cat who could be quite loving, our principal conflict remained her arbitrary abrasiveness towards the other cats. Without warning, any cat not meeting her expected standards of submissive behaviour would be subjected to her random attacks. With my background as a Feline Behaviour Consultant I would often find myself studying her. I'd never before encountered a cat masking such a compliant nature which would quickly fluctuate to indiscriminate aggressiveness. This was not typical of the "Head Cat" persona I'd experienced in my cattery but appeared to be the role that

Misty sought in our feline household.

Everything pivoted on her shifting moodiness and which one of the cats had the misfortune of crossing her path at an ill-timed moment. She would either ignore them or assume her Head Cat persona which often occurred during one of her more irritable moments. Misty did not possess the stamina or other strong personality traits deemed necessary to be an effective Head Cat. Although she was an intuitive feline, unfortunately she was also arrogant and presumptuous. She would often disappear for many hours seeking isolation in the basement, seeking the quiet and tranquility to relinquish her guard. It appeared that Misty was going to be a long-term project; she had triggered my personal need to interpret and resolve emotionally based feline behaviour issues.

Christy, on the other hand was openly affectionate with everyone; everyone that is except me. Christy was beautifully coloured, better tempered and tolerant of everyone; once again, everyone with the exception of me. Perhaps as is my tendency with cats, I'm always drawn to the one more difficult to please. I was determined to win

Christy's affections no matter how long or difficult the journey. This sister had a beautiful face, with the sides of her mouth curving upwards providing her with the expression of a permanent smile. She was a quirky, indifferent calico and had been born displaying the classic symbol of love patterned throughout her lush coat. She had lived in my home for several months before I'd noticed the distinct pattern of interlocking, colourful hearts displayed throughout her short fur. Not until one day while lying in bed as she sat on the window sill did I recognize the complexity of her colouring. It looked as if an artist had strategically placed in varied colours and configurations the complex genetic pattern of connecting hearts.

However Christy's personality did not reflect her sweetheart coat, at least not where I was concerned. She simply didn't care for my company and let her feelings be strongly known. It was going to take time to earn her respect, let alone win her feline affections. For some reason she held a grudge against me although she liked my son and was respectful to the other cats in our home. She would affectionately sit with visitors but would quickly flee from my many attempts to interact with her. I tried to ignore Christy's subtle yet snooty rebuffs which continued even after Thelma's arrival in December. I was kept at an emotional distance with our only contact remaining the simple basics of providing nourishment and maintaining a sanitary litter box. For many months that continued to be the only contact she would tolerate during our daily interactions. Perhaps she blamed me for the long plane trip from Montreal and the sudden prolonged absence of her mother. During my extended cat breeding career however I'd won over the worst natured of cats. Mind you, before that time I'd yet to experience the mystery behind the nature of a quirky calico; that was to prove an education all on its own.

Added to the mix was Mark's speaking budgie Perky that took great delight in randomly teasing our feline population.

Perky would entice her victim into the living room by imitating my tone of voice, calling them by their individual name. Perched for action on her cage, she would then take flight to systematically dive bomb them into submission. Tia, my domestic Torbie girl was frightened of Perky. If Perky was out of her cage she would fly through the house seeking Tia's company. I believe Tia's fear of the parakeet became Perky's motivator as she enjoyed landing on the cat's back whenever she'd walk across the room. When Tia sat on the back of the couch Perky would take flight, landing a respectable distance away from the cat. Perky would then proceed to tease her by slowly hopping closer until she was able to nibble Tia's paws. That was enough for my girl; Tia would flee the couch with Perky in close pursuit following her in flight as she ran from the room. Perky's fearless kamikaze antics around the cats may have been an amusing sight but one day it would also prove to be her salvation. She experienced no fear nor saw any danger from the many felines that occupied her home. However life changed for Perky when the calico girls were introduced to the house and Thelma confessed to having a terrible fear of all birds.

I soon realized that Christy had inherited an impressive ability for jumping, coupled with an equal fondness for birds in flight. Therefore not taking any chances, Christy was always placed in another room when Perky took flight. Perhaps our bird had no idea that an athletic domestic cat was capable of leaping mid air to extensive heights. Perky's past feline experiences only included respectful cobby legged Persian and Himalayan queens. This knowledge was then extended to include Tia, who had developed her fear of birds due to Perky's relentless teasing.

One evening I was working on a magazine article totally focused on completing it before bed. Mark, at ten years of age, had assumed the responsibility for cleaning his bird's cage. With the bird in her cage, he carried it to the basement for its weekly cleaning. A few minutes later I glanced up from my computer to witness Christy proudly walking into my office carrying Perky in her mouth. In an instant, with a pounding heart, I caught the cat while she held onto her trophy catch. I heard my voice saying, "Christy... let the birdie go... let the birdie go." I had my hands around the cat while the bird was struggling for her freedom. Perky was obviously angry as she assumed that cats were simply provided for her own personal amusement. Had Christy caught her in a manner that would have enabled Perky to bite back, then I'm sure the parakeet would have taken care of the situation herself.

Christy obeyed my instructions and released the bird. Perky took flight searching the house in an attempt to locate Mark and her cage. Picking Christy up, I gratefully hugged and praised her for being such a good girl. Mark entered my office obviously fearing the worst case scenario which was clearly evident by his tear-stained face. He explained how the bird had been sitting on his shoulder as she always did when her cage was being cleaned. Perky took flight and Christy leapt into the air and caught her. He was sure he'd lost his bird and came to tell me of his terrible experience. Mark couldn't believe his bird was fine. I explained that Perky was so accustomed to cats that she was more annoyed than frightened. What truly amazed me was Christy's reaction to my instructions to let the bird go. She did what many cats would never do, she listened, she understood and Perky was given her freedom. The worst thing I could have done was punish Christy for following my instructions. Instead, she was given praise and not loudly criticized for her actions.

When I told Thelma what had just transpired she attempted to hit the cat. I insisted that Christy should be praised because she had obeyed me and it was wrong to hit cats under any circumstances. Although that puzzled Thelma, she eventually accepted my reasoning and admitted that what I said made sense.

While Perky was to live a long life, this situation did not improve my relationship with Christy. I adored her for obeying me however I don't believe she saw events from my perspective. She'd gone to the trouble of catching her own dinner only to be forced to release her prey. The one time she was successful was many years later when she actually pulled a canary cage down to shatter the contents onto the floor. I wasn't to discover this catastrophic act of feline pillaging until I returned home from work later in the day. I was naturally angry because I'd lost Aviary, my beautiful male canary of many years and father to several clutches of babies. That evening while Christy laid on my lap I fought mixed emotions of loving her yet loathing her extraordinary ability to catch birds. I was determined that this situation would never occur again, with that being the last time Christy ever held any of my birds in her mouth.

Christy displaying sweet innocence;
butter wouldn't melt in her mouth

*Even if you have just destroyed a Ming Vase, purr.*
*Usually all will be forgiven.*
**- Lenny Rubenstein**

There was only one incident after Thelma's arrival when Christy acknowledged my presence in her life to be of any value. We were all home when she discovered a new game with a paper bag. Unfortunately during her play she trapped her body as she slipped through the handle of the bag. She had freedom of movement but the bag's handle became tightly caught around her middle and the bag itself made a loud frightening noise as it followed her wherever she went. She flew through the house in an escalating state of terror trying to dislodge herself. Everyone just stared at her as she panicked running from room to room with her body ensnared by the bag's handle. She may have been frightened but I knew she wasn't in any danger. Cats will reach a severe state of high anxiety during a flight or fight panic and Christy had surpassed her limits. No one dared to approach her as with her accelerating fear she was past acknowledging friend from foe. Once a cat has reached this level of panic they may bite and attack anyone attempting to assist them.

Christy sought refuge in Thelma's room and quickly realized as I followed that she had no choice; I was the only one willing to take a chance risking her fury to provide a rescue. Although well aware that Christy appeared to dislike me, she was equally aware I was the only feline caretaker in the house. She hesitated on the bed and then permitted me to restrain her while she was released from her self-imposed prison of the brown paper bag. I pulled the tight handle off her back and she was gone in a second without even a nod of appreciation for saving her. I'd like to believe perhaps it was at that moment she realized how much I cared for her; possibly she'd been left with a lasting impression that when she found herself in trouble I'd be there. While I wasn't her mother, she knew I was the one who had assumed her mother's duties. Thelma had limited sight due to her diabetes and as the months passed, she was silently enduring the onset of complete blindness.

Thelma never took me into her confidence regarding the

changes in her health but within a short period of time I realized that she had permanently lost her sight. I'm not sure if she thought I would abandon her, thinking such an additional responsibility would be too much for me. Quite possibly it was a simple matter of false pride on her behalf and I respected her privacy. We never discussed her sightless condition but I was there as her eyes when she needed me. Christy and Misty appeared to sense her dilemma as well. So as to not startle her, all our cats would approach her slowly as only a feline does when encountering anyone with such a disability.

Thelma dearly loved her calico girls. However having never owned cats before, she attempted to control her felines in the same manner as some owners discipline their dogs. She constantly raised her voice and gave them taps on their bottoms in an attempt to curb their normal feline behaviour. Although the calicos welcomed their mother's presence back into their lives, I noticed a negative altering of their behaviour.

After several weeks had passed I shared my observations of the calicos' neurotic tendencies with her. Both girls were driven with an incessant compulsive need to lick the arms of everyone who held them. Although I knew this was their manner of internalizing the scent of the person they were encountering, I also sensed they were so compelled due to their early declawing operation. Thelma would become irritated with the girls compulsively licking her arms and legs and would respond with her own loudly voiced discipline. I took the opportunity to provide advice which resulted in the desired behavioural management she needed. Without the stress from repetitive angry verbal commands her felines slowly began to adapt and change. Thelma told me that she had a better understanding of her cats in the several months we shared together than in the three years she had previously owned them. She was deeply sincere and it touched my heart that she shared this information with me during the last few weeks of her life.

Even six months after their arrival the calicos still refused to acknowledge my presence in their lives. Not only did they not appreciate my efforts to make their lives more comfortable, but they also refused my many attempts to initiate a relationship with them. I was simply put in my place and totally ignored. Although Misty would permit me to pet her on occasion, Christy's affections remained solely reserved for her owner.

As Thelma's condition worsened it became necessary for her to remain in hospital and leave the girls in my care. I promised to continue to provide care for both girls for the duration of their young lives. However as the days passed I wondered if my decision had been a wise one.

Several days following Thelma's death her beloved calicos remained confused and unsettled. I was unsure of how to comfort them while they were in emotional bereavement. We were all grieving Thelma's loss, however Misty and Christy felt abandoned and were only aware that she was no longer available to love them. The girls needed privacy so I thought it best to empty Thelma's clothing onto the bed in her room. I provided food, water and a litter box for the girls' private use in the bedroom where they had slept while Thelma lived in my home.

The two calicos had freedom of movement within the house but rarely left Thelma's room. For three weeks the girls preferred to be left in peace and slept on their deceased owner's clothing covering the entire bed. It was only after a month had passed and as I noticed the perfume from Thelma's clothing had begun to fade that the girls would leave the room for longer periods of time. Eventually when her scent was no longer present, even to a cat's sensitive nose, they finally accepted their deceased owner was truly gone.

As time passed I witnessed distinct changes in their perception of my role in their lives. Felines place great trust in their sense of smell. However once Thelma's scent had totally faded from her clothing they quickly lost interest in their private bedroom. After they completely abandoned the clothing I started occasionally using Thelma's perfume when I handled the girls. I believe this also assisted in their perception that I would be taking her place by providing care for them.

Christy was the more aloof of the two cats and for several weeks maintained her devotion to Thelma. With time though, she slowly began to transfer her loyalty to me. Eventually the long wait was over and I was rewarded with a feline's love that I'd only experienced with a few cats during my lifetime. After Thelma's passing I changed her name from Christy to Chrissy as I needed to make her my own cat. I believe softening her name may have had some reflection on her bonding and developing a relationship with me. Misty was renamed Missy, however even softening her name did not have the desired effect on her behaviour. She lived for several more years before I lost her to kidney disease and she was able to find peace with Thelma. Strangely enough though, Chrissy did not appear to grieve for the sister she had shown such devotion for during her life.

In Chrissy's new life with me she nurtured a strong maternal instinct yet it was coupled with stubborn resistance. She even extended her welcome to include a ten-week-old kitten whose personality completed our multi-cat family. Jewel, a Himalayan Blue Tortie Point kitten, was quickly accepted into the fold. Chrissy appeared quite pleased and became Jewel's mother, accepting the kitten as any mother would her own baby. This beautiful calico fills my heart on a daily basis yet still plays like a kitten herself despite her age.

As the years passed there were to be changes ahead for all of us. Chrissy played a major role by always providing her loving support on those days when I especially needed her presence the most. Although my life continued to exist with endless obstacles, I found the most comfort by simply being with my cats. Many friends couldn't accept my need for solitude nor my strong desire to be alone with only my cats for company.

I believe it's a common fear amongst women to not become the sad stereotype of a spinster. A single woman so lonely with life that she feels compelled to fill the emptiness of her home with loving felines. The young professional will also hide her deep attachment to the beloved cat waiting patiently for her arrival home come day's end. No one wants to be thought of as the cat lady, who unlucky in love and not able to manage an intimate relationship develops a preference solely for the company of felines. Although unsure if I met such a definition, I had a preference for and discovered personal serenity in the time I spent solely with my cats. I found such solitude more satisfying than the bother of dating and the uncertainty of relationships with men.

I believe that I am well liked and socially inclined by nature but professionally I have also faced the same situation. Still my friends eventually accepted that I have a need to guard my privacy. Truth be known, in my career as a writer I often prefer my own company to time shared with others. I believe that when considering my former history of working physically difficult 70-hour weeks, I spent more time away from home than was healthy. While raising my son I maintained a simple social life and was accepting of my situation. In order to survive I existed by sleeping to work and working to once again sleep. This became my life and was necessary to meet the high expectations required to raise my son. As a single mother I craved peace and solitude. When Mark was sleeping, my preference was to only share that short period of time I wasn't working with my beloved cats. Only then was I able to maintain the discipline needed to function, consumed in a life consisting of endless hours of work.

I have always accepted that nothing in life remains the same, good or bad. With the passing of years I was to welcome the man I would eventually marry into the private circle of my life. We met by chance which is often the case when something has been preordained to bless your life. Thinking back, had I any inclination of such an unexpected event, I would have been filled with anxiety and avoided that inevitable moment. I believe the Universe takes care of such matters and we became friends first before discovering our lives were meant to be shared in marriage.

Chrissy appeared aware that there was an importance to this male friend when first meeting him, as eventually were all the cats in my home. She knew he was special even before I did. I'll always remember the look of amazement on Paul's face as the cats gathered to enthusiastically greet him. He hadn't been prepared for such a thorough inspection as over the years I had seldom invited men to my home. Eventually he grew to love them as much as I did, and then we slowly grew to love each other. Within the next two years we decided to marry and I've never experienced one moment of regret. Now our lives were really going to change as Paul owned his own home and I was saying goodbye to my rented one. It was the only home my son had ever known, however Mark was now a grown man and in seeking his independence had moved to a nearby apartment the year before.

It was the week before my wedding day. I was going to be marrying the kindest, most loving and patient man I'd ever known. He was all that and much more for he was welcoming Mark and my cats into his life as well.

As sometimes occurs just when everything seems perfect, a serious problem will surface. This time, due to its medical urgency, my wedding plans would no longer be the center of my attention. That particular day, I returned home from work and had just opened the front door to my duplex. My cats were gathered on the staircase, each one occupying their own step, patiently awaiting my arrival and their personalized greeting. As had become Chrissy's routine she walked down the stairs to receive the first greeting. Before I could touch her and without warning, she squatted and urinated on the carpet. She quickly retraced her steps back up the stairs and disappeared out of sight.

Years earlier after Chrissy and I had bonded, she'd never displayed any inappropriate behavioural problems. Chrissy was a clean cat and had always used her litter box without fail. This was serious because we were about to move into Paul's beautiful home. I feared kidney failure and at twelve years of age, it would mean she was terminally ill. I would be losing her and in a sense giving her back to Thelma. This was supposed to be a joyous time in my life, I was deeply in love and finally marrying my soul mate. Now I was also possibly losing my sweetheart calico girl.

Paul and I brought her to the vet together because I feared the worst case scenario that we would be leaving the office without her. My beautiful Chrissy, my funny quirky little sweetheart of a calico; this bittersweet occurrence was happening with my wedding only two days away.

My beloved vet George had retired years earlier and knowing me well, had compassionately dealt with my sensitive nature. After working with cats for so long, when encountering my next vet I was determined to never show emotion and always remain professionally detached. In other words a professional never displays emotion and absolutely never cries when in the presence of a veterinarian. I respected my new vet and had been using his practice for several years. Chris had the same empathy and respect for his clients and their pets as George had practiced when I had my registered cattery. Chris wasn't aware of my background and as a writer of feline material this was my preference.

Chris carefully examined Chrissy and listened while I explained her recent changes in behaviour which included increased water consumption. I had only one prayer, an unexpressed wish that diabetes had once again touched my life. If this was to be his medical opinion then I would be blessed with the same gift from diabetes twice in my lifetime, and in each situation the experience involved Chrissy. He confirmed that she may indeed be diabetic but that further tests would be necessary. It was at that moment that I lost my control and burst into tears of gratitude. I started sobbing so loudly I'm sure everyone in the reception area could hear me but at that moment I didn't care. If my vet was correct then this meant with daily insulin injections Chrissy would still be mine. I'm sure Chris had seen patients cry once given this diagnosis, however never with such joy. I'd held back my attachment for my dear Chrissy for so long that I was suddenly overwhelmed with emotion. I was simply thrilled by the chance of diabetes because this meant life. Whereas if her kidneys were shutting down I would then be losing her. The blood sample was taken, the bill paid and we waited for the results which were received the morning of my wedding day. Chris confirmed that Chrissy was indeed diabetic. It was the most priceless gift I received on my wedding day. The gift of time, more precious time with my sweet calico.

My wonderful husband welcomed us all into his beautiful home. My cats suddenly had a chance to enjoy an outside balcony and enough room to chase each other up and down a long hallway. I've never felt so blessed or loved in all my life. Finally I was able to have an office in my own home and write the feline literature I'd always wanted.

Chrissy proudly assumed the role of Head Cat and in taking charge, took her many feline responsibilities to heart. She was now the senior cat of our household and patiently watched over each one of us. Her adopted kitten Jewel, now eight years old, still enjoyed the position of baby so Chrissy obliged by playing the role of her mother. Each feline adjusted to their preferred routine as the cats comfortably settled into their new home. As the only male, Tally declined attempting the role of Head Cat as it was simply too strenuous an effort. He never altered his preference for spending his days at play with the girls. Tia decided sleep was to remain her highest priority and therefore claimed the master bedroom as her personal domain. Chrissy decided that in order to keep me motivated and actively writing she would extend her status of Head Cat to also include me. She enjoyed my desk and officially became the Office Cat. Nothing pleases me more than her presence beside my computer monitor or sitting next to me snuggling in the cat bed now placed on her chair.

Left to right, Tia, Jewel and Chrissy

***In my experience, cats and beds seem to be a natural combination.***
***- Dr. Louis J. Camuti, DVM***

I remained Tally's special person but the girls often played fickle and sought my husband's affections in the evenings. Chrissy would dally back and forth by sitting on my lap one night only to abandon my affections to then favour Paul. She developed a fondness for his hands quickly tapping her entire body in a gentle massage. She became a little spoiled and rather insistent, not leaving him alone until the nightly ritual had been completed to her satisfaction. In the coolness of the early mornings she would touch his arm and he would lift the blankets for her to slip underneath the warmth of the covers. They would then sleep together for a few more hours until it was time to begin the day. I marvelled at Chrissy's ability to care for others yet aptly manage her feline timetable to meet her own needs. I was only familiar with long hours of work and she became my living example of working in moderation. She was a daily inspiration as I strove to establish direction in my wonderful new role as Paul's wife.

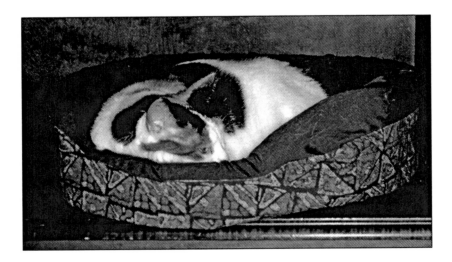

Chrissy as Head Cat, resting but maintaining the status quo

*Who among us hasn't envied a cat's ability to ignore the cares of daily life and to relax completely?*
**- Karen Brademeyer**

We took Chrissy's diabetes to heart and maintained a rigid schedule of providing insulin to our girl at 7:00 a.m. and then again at 7:00 p.m. daily. Chrissy took the new routine in stride. As with many cats she appeared accepting and forgave the mysterious ways of her owners. Chrissy knew we had her best interest at heart and despite the minor discomfort of her injection, she seemed to comprehend that we were helping her. Our calico knew the exact time of day she received her insulin and only insisted that she be awake and prepared for her injection. Being such a smart girl, she would vocalize her permission when she saw either of us holding her insulin needle.

Diabetes held one advantage for her, when we travelled it was mandatory that she always came with us. She would be in her cat carrier but often enjoyed sitting on my lap to watch the scenery pass by the car windows. Perhaps this assisted the bonding process between Chrissy and her adopted baby, our Blue Point Himalayan kitten. Jewel had required expensive eye surgery in Washington State and Chrissy always came with us for her appointments. We would be away from home for several days and Jewel needed her mother. Chrissy was a comfort to Jewel and loved to travel. She blossomed with this new routine in her life and enjoyed the perks as they came her way. Diabetes became simply another duty in my routine when providing daily care for my cat family. I remained filled with gratitude because diabetes had extended the life of my sweetheart girl. I felt blessed beyond words because no other wedding gift could have made me happier than more time with my calico.

Jewel and Chrissy back home after Jewel's surgery

In every blended family the cats will naturally adapt to a comfortable routine. When Paul and I married the girls decided to shower him with their affections. My boy Tally remained devoted to resting with me every night. Chrissy, after spending time with my husband, would always take her place resting on my lap while Tally slept on my chest. As far as I was concerned my life was beyond perfect despite the changes that were soon to follow.

My cousin Patricia and I are separated by many miles and most of our contact is by telephone or through e-mail. Although born as cousins, our relationship is so close that we are bound as tightly as any two sisters could ever be. Not having sisters ourselves, we will forever be sisters to each other. We are both cat lovers and the contents of our e-mail are filled with stories of our cats. I've kept much of her correspondence from last year because I could never duplicate the energy or emotion of this past winter. Chrissy is an amazing cat and demonstrated just how seriously she took her responsibilities when we were left without power, heat and telephone. With my sister's permission I have decided to share our correspondence as Chrissy absolutely amazed me during this particularly horrific winter storm experience.

*Dearest Patricia,*

*There is no way to tell you everything that has happened except to take you through the last week. Do you remember when I said not to expect me online for a while because we were expecting a windstorm and we would lose power? Well it was so much more than that. Before I start, I want to thank you for writing to me even though I couldn't access my e-mail. When the electricity and internet access was finally restored I was thrilled to see you'd thought of me.*

*The day we were expecting the power outage I was scrambling to write as much copy as I could for the next book because I knew it would be my last opportunity. We only have one road that connects us to Victoria and when something happens you just can't get out.*

*I've lived in Victoria most of my life and I know how strong our winds can be. Living in the country however, during bad weather, I learned that here it's often more intense than when I was living in the city. However it didn't really matter where you lived because this was the worst storm we've ever experienced.*

*The Weather Network forecasted hurricane force winds to commence around 11:00 p.m. ... precisely at 11:10 p.m. it started, and they produced a sound unlike anything I have ever heard before. By 2:00 a.m. all we could hear outside was the crashing of trees and debris around the house. We were up all night because it was too loud to sleep. The next morning you might have thought we'd been bombed outside. Of course the power was out but we'd anticipated losing that.*

*It took us several days to clear the property from all the debris. On Monday, after three days of no power, we were finally able to leave our home and travel to Victoria. As we drove the destruction was unbelievable. At least a dozen trees had fallen across the highway and were piled up along the side of the road. Many power lines had fallen and were also left at the roadside. Trees were leaning against trees and looked as if they could fall at any moment. Later we were to learn that much of the destruction was as a result of the strong rainstorms we'd been enduring this past fall season. The rainstorms weakened the roots of these huge trees and the hurricane force winds simply blew them over. A large area of British Columbia from Victoria to Vancouver experienced the same storm.*

*We had no power, no heat, no telephone and no cable. The*

*damage was so extensive that in order for the workers to do their job all the power had to be kept off. However I was praying for the men out there working for all of our comfort. They've been working non-stop since mid November. We've had about eight power outages due to weather on the island and in particular where we were situated in the country.*

*What I will never forget though is the sound of the wind. I've never heard anything like it. It was just the most unholy sound... like the devil himself was creating havoc outside. All the cats were patrolling the house because they knew we were in a dangerous situation. Jewel, my baby, was trying her best to open the window to see outside... that's just like Jewel. She knew something exciting was happening and she didn't want to miss any of the action. I opened the front door during the storm to personally witness the fury of the winds. It was grey and loud, the force from the wind flung the door from my hands. I rescued my cast iron cat that sits on the outside porch railing, I was shocked it was still there. So for now that's how I have spent the last week. Freezing cold and without any of the amenities that in the past I never appreciated as much as I do now. I've never been in a situation where everything is gone, power, telephone and cable. That's something I will never forget.*

*Of all the cats Chrissy was more concerned with our welfare than her own comfort. I was trying in vain to keep her under the down comforter to stay warm with the other cats. However this didn't suit Chrissy who seriously respected her role as the resident Head Cat. Despite her age and short coat, although she felt the bitter coldness of the house more than any of the others, she also felt the need to protect us. Chrissy knew the circumstances of her home were beyond our control and took it upon herself to make regular patrols from one end of the house to the other. Whenever she came near me I did my best to keep her under the covers in an attempt to warm her. Most of the time Paul was more successful because she dearly loved being close to him. It didn't seem to matter though as she would patrol the house for ten to fifteen minutes every hour around the clock. She is such an amazing cat, I guess it shows how much I respect and adore her.*

*I'm just grateful that a tree didn't hit our house... so many people have lost their homes. Again I believe God has been watching over us yet once again.*

*Well now I'd better get to work but I have one more thing to tell you. We have just been informed that another storm is coming in and should hit us sometime tomorrow. We will be going out to get supplies because this is also supposed to be a bad one. So once again Pat, if you don't hear from me you will know why. We appear to be living in a weather war zone right now... the trees around us are like missiles. I don't know what will happen but this is how life is at the moment. Please keep in touch. I have kept all your e-mail and will answer them individually as the days pass if we have power. I started writing a snail mail letter to you but realized that at this time of the year we'd probably have the internet back before you ever received it. Never forget that I love you. Thank you for being there.*

*Much love always,*
*xoxo j*

We survived the winter storms and I was left with a strong connection to Chrissy's determination in caring for us.

Patricia and I have exchanged daily e-mails for so many years that despite the distance and years apart, we understand each other very well. I promised that if I ever wrote a book of cat stories then I dearly wanted to record the life of her beautiful male.

**121**

When Patricia lost her tuxedo boy of many years I grieved the loss with her. I would hold my Tally and feel the weight of Chrissy on my lap thanking the Universe for my many blessings. At the time however I was blissfully unaware of the changes ahead. Several months later my world was tainted when Chrissy suddenly became quite ill. Within a few days I was forced to accept, after many years of her loving care, that our time was coming to an end. As Paul and I coped with her illness I was only comfortable sharing this difficult period of loss with Pat. She was still mourning her own boy and I was grateful that she understood my situation so well. As a writer I prefer to use my personal correspondence with Pat for there are no better words to express how I was feeling and exactly how the events transpired.

*My dearest sister,*

*I'm not even going to ask how are you today. I know how you are only too well. I'm writing this as I'm getting strong feelings that you're at the vet's right now with your beloved Chrissy. It's just so sad, even though she has had a wonderful life, I understand your sadness, trust me. I'm just so sorry about Chrissy, I share in your pain and your loss is also mine now. At least she's going to meet Barney now. I'm sure they'll be the best of friends, look at who their mother's are.*

*I don't even know if you'll read this today, it doesn't matter, whenever will be just fine. I remember that awful day when taking Barn to the vet, I just needed to come on here, I just wanted to tell you about my horrendous day. I knew you would have words of re-assurance, even though we did the only thing we had left to do.*

*Again, just know how sorry and sad I am about your darling Chrissy.*

*P.xxx*

*Dearest Pat,*

*When you were writing your e-mail we were at the vet's and it was received while I was holding Chrissy's lifeless body driving back home. I love you and thank you from the bottom of my heart. I can't do much today... I'm sipping an Australian Shiraz at the moment... it was a touch of gin on the weekend. Not a lot... ever since I've known we were going to lose her I needed just enough to ease my nerves and see me through. Give me 24 hours and I'll be able to respond. Chrissy has already told me she likes where we have placed her body... I'll tell you more tomorrow.*

*As always, xoxo j*

*Hi my dearest sister,*

*You have been so in my thoughts today, I know you'll be missing Chrissy badly, I know you will be feeling lost without her, even though you gave her such a wonderful life.*
*It's far from easy accepting they really have gone. It's reassuring that she approves of her final resting place, tell me more whenever you're able. No rush at all just take your time. So you would have been at the vet's the time I had such strong*

*feelings you were.*

*We went out for dinner tonight, how I enjoy doing that so much. It's a nice country pub in a small picturesque village, about eight miles from here. On the way there, I always think of you as there are many small churches with such old gravestones, I bet you would just love them and one day I'll show them to you. Just know you're in my thoughts and my heart. When you're hurting then I am as well. When I know you're content with life then it makes me content as well.*

*Love you, take care,*
*Pat*

*Dearest Pat,*

*I am writing of Chrissy's life as a chapter in "Every Cat Has A Story" which is slowly but surely taking shape and form. If you want Barney's in this edition we will have to work together.*

*Unless you have lost a cat whom you have loved for many years how can you know how someone feels? I am still emotionally raw and am having problems focusing. I will be writing the entire story... I actually thought I could do it here in my e-mail to you but I just can't. Paul wanted to bury Chrissy in the back garden but I knew she would rather be in the front where she can watch us come and go and see the activity of the neighbourhood. That was her nature... her quirky calico nature. I don't like burying my cats... hate it actually... placing them in the ground where I can no longer feel their presence. Somehow with Chrissy though, it seemed like the right thing to do. I've told Paul that if we are still living here and Jewel should pass then she should be placed next to her mother.*

*Chrissy was always like a mother to her. Jewel would seek her company wanting to be cleaned and they often would sleep side by side. Whereas Chrissy was also known as the Runaway Bride, Jewel would have been her bridesmaid. They both loved the outside and escaped several times.*

*Tally is my baby and so is Tia, neither would take to a burial. I swear they would haunt me to get back into their bedroom. I will have them privately cremated when the time comes... God willing, it'll be many years ahead. I was staring out of my bedroom window where I couldn't see the grave but the shovel we used was still leaning against the entrance to our house. The sight of the shovel left me cold but I knew Paul would be removing it soon. Then I saw a feline displaying all of her calico beauty pause by the front stairs. I went to the front door and saw this same beautiful calico walk across Chrissy's grave and up along the entrance to another home's property. This lovely girl had frightened me a year earlier when we were coming home as I spotted her by the side of the road. My immediate fear was Chrissy, our Runaway Bride, had escaped and been out all day while we were shopping. She was a calico but was not as colourful as Chrissy and she was also a little smaller. The face was the same however and that's what startled me so much. Although our neighbour's cats sometimes come onto our property, this little calico had never done so before.*

*I watched her, thinking, oh my there she is. For the next hour she came and went several times. The fourth time she was sighted I called Paul over to see because I simply couldn't believe it. In my heart I'd like to believe that Chrissy was saying she knew how much she was being missed. She liked being with the sister she had lost years ago and was also back with Thelma. It was almost like a thank you which was delivered by the little calico's unexpected presence. I keep on looking for her now but she hasn't returned... she had a message to deliver and has no need to come back. That was the first visitation.*

*We had brought Chrissy to the vet wrapped in a blanket that normally lies in one of the cat beds in the bedroom. Jewel used to lie in that cat bed but lost interest, as cats do, after a month or two. When we arrived home from the vets I placed the blanket back in the bed. Just as I was getting up this morning Jewel was in the cat bed pawing the blanket that had held Chrissy. It startled me because she had shown no interest in this blanket or bed for over a year. She looked at me and I started crying because I knew what she was doing. She sensed that her mother was missing. Although she can be snooty and detached sometimes, Jewel will show her affectionate nature when the mood suits her. There was no caterwauling throughout the house from the remaining cats, but Jewel let me know this morning that something was wrong and she knew her mother was missing. Jewel now appears far more serious, almost sombre; she now walks through the house with an air of recent sorrow.*

*I have a lot to share with you but these are just a few references for me to draw upon when I'm writing her story. I asked Paul what he remembered most about our calico girl and he replied, "She took such good care of us... she was the boss and mothered us all." Although she took care of her own needs, we were important to her as well. Do you remember when I told you how she would run through the house when we lost power after being left in the dark and cold to make sure everything was alright? We couldn't stop her, she'd only come back when she was chilled to the bone to lie beside Paul. Within the hour she would patrol the house again making sure we were safe. That is what I remember the most about her. I was concerned with keeping her warm while she was more concerned about the safety of the house and maintained her hourly patrols. Chrissy was the epitome of the Sociable Independent personality as mentioned in my last book, "How to Hide Your Cat From the Landlord."*

*I don't believe anyone, unless they are a devoted cat lover, would appreciate how this loss and my grief are affecting me. I said two rather bizarre things to my husband last night. I was worried about Chrissy alone and cold in her grave and voiced my concern. Strangely enough Chrissy's favourite flannel sheet finally had a tear so large in it that we couldn't use it on the bed any longer. I washed it thinking maybe I would eventually use it for dusters. The cats all loved that sheet and I knew they would miss it on the bed. Paul suggested that we use the sheet for Chrissy's burial. So last night when I asked him, "Do you think she's cold out there all alone?" he replied, "No, she's warmly wrapped up in her favourite sheet and she's content." Later that evening I asked him, "Do you think Chrissy knows how much we loved her?" He wisely commented that yes he believed she did know... Jewel answered that question for me this morning by sitting in the cat bed, she knew I needed some tangible proof.*

*I'm going to send this now Pat because I'm fading fast. I thought you might find this interesting and you'll have a chance to read more of Chrissy's story when I'm able to think more clearly.*

*Love you, xoxo j*

While Pat and I were writing Barney's story **The Green Pawed Moggie**, Chrissy had been incredibly strong and well. Every morning she was either sitting in front of the monitor blocking the view of the screen or was sleeping in her chair next to my desk. We never know when we will lose our beloved cats, and perhaps with the emotions that are involved when enduring such a loss that's for the best. I've always thought the only problem with cats is that their wonderful lives

**127**

are never long enough. Each precious feline soul that graces our world has a specific time to work their loving magic within their families. I know that my Sweetheart girl has left a permanent mark on my heart, she left no work unfinished during her life.

Several weeks ago we passed an elderly lady holding the little calico that delivered Chrissy's message on the day we buried her. I wanted to stop the car but my husband was driving. I don't believe even if I'd been alone in the car I would have mustered the courage to speak to her. I wanted to know her little girl's name because I felt it should be included in this book. I rarely see this lovely calico, but every time I do it's as if Chrissy is letting me know she is alright and still staying nearby protecting her family.

It wasn't until a week prior to publication that the synchronicity of the little calico's situation was presented to validate Chrissy's memory. My husband met her owner by chance and was given her name. Bunny lives with her sister Missy and both are calicos. That was enough for me, little Bunny and Missy are calico sisters just as my Chrissy and Missy had been. I do believe Bunny's presence was there that difficult day to somehow comfort me.

Of all the stories I've written for this book Chrissy's has been the most difficult. I believe I blocked out many of her memories because they were just too painful. We had a power outage in our area last week, a grim reminder of last winter. Our power company is pruning the tress in our area before the next winter season arrives. I was forced to take time away from my computer and decided to prepare material for the next book I will be writing. However I couldn't concentrate and instead spent that time reflecting on Chrissy. I sat on the front porch and was facing Chrissy's grave. After her burial I had placed my favourite blue stone cat I'd purchased on Salt Spring Island to clearly mark her final resting place. I spoke to her, heart to heart, as only a cat lover will during intimate moments of remembering. Those two days without power connected me to my most precious memories of Chrissy, touching my heart once again. She helped me to complete her story as I had been struggling, attempting to capture the essence of such a vibrant calico.

Pat and I have always shared our most private thoughts and feelings. She gave me great peace of mind thinking her darling Barney and my Chrissy were playing together as time and distance no longer mattered in their world. Pat and I have been separated by 6,000 miles and more years than we care to remember. To have lost our cats within several months became yet another bond we shared. If I hadn't lost Chrissy in the middle of writing this book then professionally I never would have acknowledged my relationship with Pat as my beautiful sister/cousin who I one day hope to meet in person. Pat and I have felt it best to place her *Green Pawed Moggie* next to this story of my own sweet Chrissy. When it comes to the loss of a beloved cat I believe grief becomes the greatest equalizer. Pet lovers instinctively respect the emotional journey necessary for each one of us to endure after we've encountered such a loss.

Enough time has passed that Pat is now comfortable sharing her life with another cat. She is being careful and her search continues as she is waiting for just the right one to speak to her heart. Of course I'm not as wise as my sister because I wanted another calico and almost purchased one at a TICA cat show several months ago. My patient husband sat with me while I held a precious exotic calico kitten trying to convince myself it would be alright with time. My wise husband was quiet but silently shook his head, convincing me I was still suffering from grief with a bad case of Kitten Fever thrown in for good measure.

After owning cats for so many years I really should have known better but the heart wants what the heart wants. Although I am writing a series of books on buying and breeding purebred kittens I ignored one very important rule. Pat knew to have another tuxedo boy would be unfair to her memory of Barney. As she puts it quite well, "He's going to be a tough act to follow." Chrissy was also a once in a lifetime experience. Where on earth could I find such a loving combination of a feline soul so filled with both fire and affection? So now I sadly realize that it may be many years before I hold another calico kitten in my arms. I have learned that sometimes the most worthwhile experiences in life happen when you are least expecting them, and sometimes you are blessed with a living miracle. This was my experience with diabetes. Chrissy gave me the most precious gift I could have ever hoped for on my wedding day. I was given the blessing of additional time with my beautiful and quirky calico girl.

Chrissy's story has been difficult to write, and even more difficult to find the right sentiment to create the perfect ending. In touching those places within the heart, tracing memories from such an amusing character as she was, I was simply never pleased with the results. Every time I thought the ending was adequate to express my affection for my beloved girl, upon closer examination I was never quite satisfied.

I've decided the best way to conclude this story is to relay the incidents around the day I was actively attempting to complete the final paragraph. Jewel sauntered into my office, as she often does, and began her familiar caterwauling when demanding a visit with her beloved canaries. I've learned that the only way to silence her is to abandon my work and carry her to the birds we keep in my husband's office. Safe from harm, the bird cage has been placed too high for Jewel to enjoy unless she is held to monitor her viewing. A son and daughter remain to entertain my Himalayan, born from a clutch of canaries Aviary fathered prior to becoming Chrissy's last canary dinner.

On such vocal occasions Jewel draws upon her inherited Siamese voice, becoming increasingly louder in an attempt to have her needs met. I need peace and quiet when I write but I've given up trying to silence her because nothing works when she wants to visit the canaries. On this day I was particularly keen to finish the final paragraph however I left my desk and walked down the hall for Jewel to enjoy her birds. She will usually be satisfied after one of her canary visitations and will leave me in peace to continue writing. However I was mistaken because it wasn't time with the canaries that she was seeking. After ten minutes of watching the birds I placed Jewel on the floor and returned to my desk. She followed me back to my office and continued loudly crying as though deliberately attempting to distract me from my work. She varied from sitting in front of my monitor which is something she's never done in the past, to sitting in the chair beside my desk that had belonged to her mother. Although a month had now passed since my experience with Jewel that day, I felt compelled to rewrite the ending. As I reflect back it appeared as if Jewel sensed I was writing about Chrissy. I was emotional to be sure, but Jewel did as she had never done before, much in the same manner as her mother had always done before her. She remained with me for the rest of the afternoon, watching as I completed Chrissy's story.

Recently Jewel has developed a little cowlick on top of her head which sticks out providing her with a rather comical expression. I'd like to think that somehow Chrissy is still with us, an ever patient presence as my beautiful calico office cat. Jewel has never returned to my office with the exception of occasionally wanting to visit with her birds. However I'd like to believe that Chrissy's presence was there the day I was trying to complete her story. Perhaps she wasn't pleased with my writing and spoke to me through Jewel's presence. Jewel's cowlick has developed during the time I have been working on Chrissy's story. Even though I'm the one who grooms the cats I never noticed and it was my husband who first brought it to my attention. I'm sure the cowlick that Jewel now proudly displays is evidence that Chrissy remains nearby as Jewel loved Chrissy cleaning her head. At least that's what I'd like to believe after endless unsuccessful combings trying to return Jewel's fur to its former glory.

I had so wanted to conclude Chrissy's story with a literary touch of class but as our Head Cat, classy simply wasn't Chrissy's style. With Jewel's assistance I hope I've now given her memory the justice it deserves. Jewel's little cowlick and love for birds is only one of the new calico traits she has recently adopted. Every now and then my gentle Himalayan will surprise me by performing one of her mother's quirky calico antics. It happens when least expected and through the most unlikely of sources as a small, quiet Himalayan. Jewel's snooty indifference can only be compared to the treatment that Chrissy gave me when she first arrived in my home. I also find it comforting that every now and then Jewel will prowl through the house with a greater sense of purpose, much as her mother did before her. I do believe Chrissy would be so proud of her little Himi daughter. I just know my sweetheart calico will always be remembered, this especially being true when the winds howl and Jewel assumes her mother's role of protecting our home. Jewel still enjoys her nightly patrols, forever seeking those feline quests that go bump in the night. Sometimes I sense Chrissy's comforting presence is also nearby, still patiently and lovingly watching over us and diligently protecting her family.

Jewel

*I believe cats to be spirits come to earth.*
*A cat, I am sure, could walk on a cloud without coming through.*
**- Jules Verne**

# Claire's Love for Her Feral Kittens

*A home without a cat, and a well-fed, well-petted*
*and properly revered cat, may be a perfect home, perhaps,*
*but how can it prove its title?*
*- Mark Twain*

This story is taken from Jasmine Kinnear's Feline Forum on her Confessions of a Cat Breeder web site:
www.confessionsofacatbreeder.com

*Claire writes – February 23$^{rd}$...*

I am from England and am hoping someone can help! I have just got two kittens from a rescue centre; they are brother and sister and are not used to being around people. They are frightened and we cannot seem to get close enough to cuddle them. It's been nearly a week since we got them and although one of them seems to have started showing signs of improvement - if we so much as put a finger towards them they huddle together in a corner of the room. My fiancé and I are so wanting the bonding process to work and we want the kittens to start feeling loved in their new home! Do you have any ideas about how we can help two very timid nine-week-old kittens to be a little braver?

Claire

*Jasmine's Reply – February 28<sup>th</sup>...*

I've been anxious to respond with a complete consultation due to the importance of this subject. Feral kittens are not only dear to me, but the taming of their feral behaviour is also a particular interest of mine.

When you received the kittens from the rescue centre, were you informed if they were from a feral background? You have not provided this vital piece of information which would greatly assist in providing an accurate consultation. Due to your description of the brother and sister and their timid behaviour, I am going to assume that they are both feral or have a feral lineage.

Have you given them names yet? What is their colouring? What diet are you presently using and who is feeding them? Are they using their litter boxes appropriately and where have the boxes been placed for the kittens? What cat litter have you chosen to use? Have you provided them with a cat scratching pole with a high sleeping ledge for their use? Although these appear to be simple details, they are most helpful to me in ascertaining the right steps for you to follow as the kittens adjust to their new environment.

Bonding with a receptive, purring kitten is effortless, very much like falling in love. However, the situation with ferals is more complicated and requires an owner with immense patience residing in a stress-free environment. Bonding with ferals may lead to periods of frustration and can often appear as a futile waste of an owner's time. There are several procedures to follow when feral kittens are introduced into a new home.

When initiating the relationship, an owner must maintain a continuity of routine around the kitten. Feral kittens will pass through several behavioural stages of development to which the owner must adhere and accept prior to gaining the feline's affections. Trust is the first and most important rule necessary for a feral to relinquish their guard and desire contact with their owner. A delicate balance of daily contact will depend on the kitten's level of fear and responsiveness. When it comes to feral kittens, this first rule must be acknowledged before they will ever permit their person to touch them. As an owner, you will be providing unconditional love from a distance, and yet be receiving little back in return for an undetermined length of time. However, it is essential for a feral to develop a sense of trust before they will respond or accept contact with their person.

Once a foundation of trust has been established, much will depend on the individual personality of each feral as to when they will interact with their owner. Every feral is responsive to a degree but will adapt within their own timetable; therefore some kittens will take much longer than others. Nevertheless the rewards are deeply intense and the resulting relationship will be unlike any you have shared with any cat in your past. Due to the importance of feral kittens, I am going to provide an in depth feline consultation once you have replied.

I also had a feral kitten in my home, and our Tia was provided with the specific care necessary to enable her to develop into a beautiful and affectionate adult. I could not picture my life without her. Trust me, the rewards you will be receiving in the future are priceless.

May you both be blessed for the unconditional patience and care you are providing to these kittens through the next couple of weeks. I look forward to your reply on our Feline Forum and will quickly provide a response.

Always, Jasmine Kinnear
Feline Behaviour Consultant

*Claire's Reply – March 2$^{nd}$...*

The kittens: we do not know if they are feral. I wondered it myself. They do use their litter boxes correctly and are eating okay. They eat kitten food and seem to love it, and drink water. Their colouring is black and white and we are still trying to think of some appropriate names.

They have a scratching post, although we cannot easily introduce them to it as they get too nervous if we try to pick them up. Since I posted the original query, I have managed to pick one of them up and cuddle her a little, however she got nervous again and started struggling. My fiancé also managed to stroke the other one on his head, between his ears. They started playing with a little ball we provided and some string which has got to be a good sign, and they do have a high ledge to sleep on!

Hope this provides you with the information you need.

Claire

*Jasmine's Reply – March 7$^{th}$...*

Thank you for your quick response. I will now try to answer some of your questions although I will require additional information. I am going to assume that both the brother and sister are feral and my consultation will be based on that assumption.

You have indicated that they are eating kitten food. What brand of kitten food are you providing for them? Are they on both a wet and dry diet? It is always best to use a high quality kitten food, however considering their background it now becomes even more essential. It is also important that I know which of you is feeding them and your manner of informing them when dinner is served.

I believe that the kittens will eventually name themselves. It is important however to not provide them with names which may reflect any negative aspect of their personalities. As they are presently displaying skittish tendencies do not give them a name that reflects any negative energy. A calming and soothing name will be best for both the male and female kitten.

Feral kittens have a passion for cat litter and especially love playing in it. Feral cats are also known for being fastidiously clean and will use their litter appropriately. I have had very few consultations for well adjusted cats from a feral background not using their litter boxes. It is highly important to keep their boxes very clean. A feral feline is accustomed to using the outside environment and always selects a clean area. This practice must also be duplicated indoors, therefore clean the boxes at least twice a day. Have you tried a sanitary clumping litter? It would not only keep your home freshly scented but your kittens will be delighted by the familiar texture beneath their paws while in the box. Where have the boxes been placed and how many are you presently using? Where are the kittens sleeping at night?

The most difficult yet essential period of bonding with your kittens begins by gaining their trust. I know it will be difficult during this process but resist the temptation to pick up either of the kittens. They have been placed in a strange environment and have lost their mother and littermates. Presently they are not comfortable in an enclosed space and feel they have lost control of their environment. It's important to understand that your size and behaviour are foreign to them but remember you have the advantage of having assumed their mother's role. Be prepared to provide many months of unconditional love and nurturing to allow them the comfort of time necessary to promote bonding with you. However, the kittens will set the pace and you must work within their comfort zone and restrictions.

When lifting them they may become fearful with the natural flight or fight instinct coming into play. As you stop lifting them they will learn to relax and become accustomed to only your soft voice affectionately speaking to them. Once the fear of one kitten being lifted away from the other lessens, you have started working on the first level of gaining their trust.

Any attempt to play or close contact with either kitten should not involve sudden movements or they may once again become fearful of their environment and your large size. Rest assured the kittens are curious and want to interact with both of you. Once they are comfortable with your voice gently speaking to them, allow them the additional pleasure of meeting you by assuming the cat to cat posture. Lie on your stomach on the floor nearby and continue speaking to them in a quiet voice. As you are no longer invading their personal space by lifting them they will be anxious to internalize your personal scent. It may take several attempts but if you continue to lie on the floor, you have reduced your size and they should become curious to meet you. The kittens will slowly approach once satisfied that you will not make any sudden movements and they should then venture tentatively to your face. Do not extend your hand to pet them. You are now being approached as if you were also a part of their intimate feline family. The kittens should begin by touching your nose with their noses, this is virtually the kitten kiss of acceptance.

This will be a gradual occurrence with their developing trust or remaining fear of you dictating their progress, be patient as this may not occur for a while. However, if you begin every evening by lying down and welcoming their interaction they will be comforted by the routine. Trust me, the kittens are as anxious to accept you as you are to bond with them. If you give them the gift of time coupled with your love and acceptance, the bonding will naturally occur. Eventually the kittens will be climbing all over you. Following a game of play with each other, using your body as a toy, they will eventually curl up and sleep next to you. At this moment you will know that you are loved and have been accepted as a member of their feline family. As they grow, your lap will become the most treasured place in the house and there will be stiff competition for that cherished position.

Feral kittens love to play and a tall climbing pole with small platforms provides many uses. With such a pole the kittens should never scratch your furniture. They also know their personal kitty gym has been provided by you for their play and enjoyment. Another level of trust has been gained as they will interpret your kindness as understanding their need for exercise with the security of height.

They sense their importance in your life and you will be recognized for more than just providing their food. It is most important to allow the kittens to discover and explore the new pole without any interaction from you. The kittens will slowly begin to play on the pole, batting each other from one level to the next as they comfortably adjust to their new home. Although this activity may not be displayed for your personal enjoyment, rest assured it will be to your advantage eventually. Once the kittens are comfortable they will start openly playing on their pole while you are home. If you are not considered a threat they will eventually welcome your interaction during a play session. There are many toys available whereby the kittens can bat at a cat toy suspended by a pole which is held while you play with them. Once they are playing with you in this manner you have been welcomed even closer into their world of trust. Kittens learn through play and a loving owner taking such precious time to bond with them is more quickly accepted.

I have had the pleasure of owning two feral cats. The very first cat I ever owned, although totally feral, was extremely affectionate from the moment I received him. Years later I adopted a domestic five-week-old kitten we named Tia. Although the litter was sired by a feral male the mother was a domestic pet. According to her owner the domestic mother had always been rather aloof. Given a little time and patience I advised that once altering the mother she would eventually become more demonstrative with her affections.

Unfortunately for several years Tia's manner consistently mirrored the same feral behaviour of your two kittens. I tried for many months to gain her affections, however she preferred my son's distant company and totally ignored me. I dedicated time and took advantage of first understanding her before attempting any behaviour modification. She was limited in her preference of interacting with me however despite her aloofness I realized she was truly more fearful than feral. It was rather insulting as a professional to have my feral cat leave a room whenever I entered.

It took about eight months of slowly gaining her trust and never lifting her. Years later she now permits me to lift her whenever I want, however if she shows any displeasure I immediately put her down. Allowing your kittens control over their movements is very important. You want to project love and acceptance and never be considered a threat within the safe territory of their home.

If they enjoy petting then again follow their body language and only pet them while they are comforted by your touch. By permitting your kittens the freedom to set the pace of your bonding, you are not only gaining their trust but also their feline respect.

As I have indicated the rewards to come are numerous. These precious kittens will never forget the hunger or cold they encountered in their feral environment. They will learn to associate love, warmth and nourishment solely with your presence. I promise that your patience will be rewarded with a feline devotion you may never have encountered before.

Once you have answered the above questions I will complete your consultation.

Always,
Jasmine

*Claire's Reply – March 14th...*

The kittens currently sleep in the kitchen; we wanted them to get used to one room in the house at a time. This is where they are fed and where their litter box is kept so therefore we thought they would be most at ease there. They are feeding on both a wet and dry diet, both myself and my fiancé feed them, using food which is the UK's top selling brand specially designed for kittens. To let them know that food is ready, we tap on the side of their bowls. The litter box is cleaned daily and we use a clumping litter.

Over the weekend we spoke to them in a soft voice and one of them is starting to play with toys and with us. She is coming closer to us and even rubbed her nose on my fiancé's. We really think progress has been made. I heard a gentle purr from her, although this didn't last too long. Her brother is still more timid and although he plays with his sister, he still waits for us to be a substantial distance away.

The following morning the female kitten started making even more progress; she stood by me whilst I fed her breakfast, but is still nervous if I put my hand toward her.

I will, from now on though, take your advice and will not lift them for a while to see what happens.

Thanks,
Claire

*Jasmine's Reply – March 18<sup>th</sup>...*

Congratulations on the progress that you have made with the kittens. I'm going to give you a few additional words of advice to encourage these babies to adapt to their loving home.

As they are sleeping in the kitchen it becomes important that they associate their security and comfort with your presence and scent. I would suggest that each of you surrender an article of warm clothing that you have recently worn for the babies to use in their bedding. The cat's world is dominated by odours using marking scents and in this manner you will become an accepted part of their scent territory. When the kittens clean themselves, known as autogrooming, they will actually be "tasting" you through their contact with the bedding. The kittens will also be reading your scent signals when they are grooming each other, known as allogrooming. Allogrooming is a mutually affectionate gesture between the kittens indicating their closeness while they ingest each other's scent.

Eventually the two of you will be included in this fragrance exchange once you are able to touch them. Your kittens will actually enjoy "tasting you" from the scent of your sweat glands. You have mentioned that your fiancé scratched the male between his ears. Cats enjoy this area as it's a difficult area for them to reach. Ultimately they will both permit tickling and rubbing behind the ears as your scent is incorporated into their personal family scent. I would suggest that you rotate the clothing they have been given and replace it with other clothing worn by both of you on a regular basis. This enables the kittens to more quickly respond to you as your scent will remain within their personal space.

As both kittens are fearful of an outstretched hand, resist the temptation to pet them during this initial phase of bonding. I also strongly suggest that neither of you pick them up until

**143**

they are totally comfortable within your home. I did not lift my feral cat for about eight months until Tia had totally lost her fear of me. When the cats are comfortable and will sleep next to you at night or will sit with you while you are working or watching a movie you may then attempt this contact. If the cat again shows discomfort place her down and she will accept that even in your arms she has freedom of movement. You are providing unconditional love for both felines by demonstrating total respect and acceptance of their special needs.

If you are not already doing so, in addition to tapping their food dish may I suggest that you call both of them in a loving manner. Once suitable names have been chosen, use this opportunity to call them by their names. Kittens learn their names more quickly if food has been integrated as a part of the introduction.

Please keep us posted on your progress. It may be time consuming but both kittens are going to be extremely affectionate as you took the time they required for bonding.

Always, Jasmine

*Claire's Reply – March 30<sup>th</sup>...*

Last night one of the kittens touched my nose with hers! She started to purr as well, although still nervous I feel that she is making great progress. As for the other one, he still hisses when we go near and is still fearful of us. I'm hoping that as his sister gets braver, he too will start to make progress!

Thanks for all your help Jasmine, Claire

**When your kitty purrs to you,**
**doesn't it break your heart that you can't purr back?**
**- Candea Core-Starke**

*Jasmine's Reply – April 3$^{rd}$...*

Thank you for the update on your kittens. It is wonderful that you are working within the restrictions both kittens need in order to bond with you.

It has been my experience that male kittens are usually more curious about their surroundings. Females prefer their male littermates to explore their territory before attempting that great adventure themselves.

Although it is more common, however that is not always the case and says much about the developing personality of your female. When a female kitten, especially a feral one, interacts with her adopted mother she is showing great promise of the love locked within her little feline heart. I would select a name that demonstrates her affectionate but bold nature. Names from the earth such as Tara, Tessa or anything that is comfortable for you and reflects her loving nature would be suitable. It is also important to name the kittens as soon as possible because they will understand that they truly have a place in your home.

I wouldn't be concerned regarding the constant fear the little male is presently demonstrating. He is also involved with the interaction by observing his sister as she communicates her love and affection with you.

Although presently not displaying the same receptiveness as the female, he is internalizing your affection for her. Your male is also well aware of now living with warmth, comfort and a fully satisfied stomach. Only his mother was able to provide him with such security when he was a very young kitten, and eventually that affection will be transferred to you. Feral cats always require additional time to process any changes in their lives.

It is my personal experience that feral cats, once bonded and comfortable in their homes, dislike even the most minimal of changes. My very first cat was a feral five-week-old kitten who was presented to me as totally affectionate and tame. As an adult however his feral nature became more apparent. He would become terribly distraught if I made any changes within my home. If a refrigerator door was left open he would awaken me in the middle of the night to close it. If I simply moved a mirror to another location in our home he would meow for hours until it was returned to its original position. The adult feral cat I presently own hid for a week in our heating ducts while our roof was being replaced. Her feral nature was triggered due to the noise from the roofers and strong smell from the tar. Feral cats are born with exceptionally acute senses. They are also easily unsettled by unknown sounds and odours. My female, Tia, does not like me to wear any perfume and will give me a disgusted flip of her tail and state her disapproval should I even have a glass of wine with dinner. She knows my personal scent and when I alter that familiar scent she refuses to have anything to do with me.

Your male kitten may not permit affectionate interaction with you until after he has been altered. Although he accepts both of you he will remain slow in trusting his instincts to physically demonstrate his affectionate nature. Within the next several months your female will be literally walking all over you. Permit your male the luxury of time to accept that he is loved just as he is and the rewards will be many. Your female will enjoy the fact that she is the center of your world and will be very demonstrative when she interacts with either of you.

Your male will experience a separation from home to be surgically altered but will be comforted by returning to familiar surroundings. Once he is emotionally stable he should quickly duplicate his sister's affection for you. He may never be as demonstrative as she is but he should become totally dedicated to loving you and his home. I believe that his sister will not appreciate his new found boldness and will react with great displays of meowing when he wants affection from you. However she will adjust and her jealousy should only last for a short period of time.

Neither kitten may be comfortable with visitors with the exception of possibly other cat lovers who will provide some gentle attention to them. The cats will probably disappear when visitors first arrive but will soon make their presence known with your quieter friends.

Adopting a feral kitten is a lesson in love and patience. The rewards are boundless, the love exchanged remarkable. Feral cats, if kept indoors and routinely see a vet, are often healthier and tend to have longer, more satisfying lives.

Have you selected any names for your kittens? Perhaps you would like some suggestions from other cat lovers that visit our Forum? Again Claire, thank you for taking these two little darlings into your home and providing them with such tender loving care.

Always, Jasmine

*Claire's Reply – April 10th...*

It would be great to get suggestions on names for my kittens; two names that go well together and suit these babies. They are black and white and almost identical. The male has a white tip on his tail while the female's tail is completely black. However she has white legs with a black patch on one. Other than that they look the same.

Thanks again for all your help,
Claire

*Jasmine's Reply – April 27th...*

Have you named the kittens yet? I have a list of names but thought you may benefit from looking at a very long list which can be found using the Yahoo search engine: www.yahoo.com, under the search category simply place the words: cat names. There is a wonderful selection of names provided and much better than any we were able to produce. It is with total embarrassment that I don't provide our Office suggestions. I really loved the mystical cat name site provided by the Yahoo search engine. This site is wonderful and may entice you and others searching for the perfect kitten name.

Please give our readers an update on the kittens when you can.

Warm regards,
Jasmine

*Claire's Reply – July 23rd...*

Sorry I've not been in touch for a while, I've been away for a bit. Anyway, my kittens are now completely changed. We named them Shadow and Heidi, as one of them likes to hide and the other is constantly in his sibling's shadow.

Heidi, the female, is now a normal kitten, into everything and causing havoc. She is more adventurous than her brother. Shadow is still timid with strangers but wherever his sister is... he is.

He is loving towards us. In fact he's more placid than Heidi is. He jumps on our bed and rolls over waiting to have his stomach tickled.

They both sleep with us at night now, purring away gently throughout the night. They have started going outside and running around our garden. They have had their vaccinations against flu, etc. and last week both were neutered.

I am pleased that both of them have gone from hating humans to being so loving. We don't regret having them for a moment and I would like to thank you, Jasmine, for all your advice – the hard work we put into these feral kittens has paid off!

Claire

> *I love cats because I love my home*
> *and after a while they become its visible soul.*
> **- Jean Cocteau**

*Jasmine's Reply – August 1*<sup>*st*</sup>*...*

Dear Claire,

When feral kittens enter a loving home it is truly the essence of their owners that determines their developing personalities.

For your babies to have come so far means they were accepted despite their initial fearful and timid nature. By providing unconditional love the kittens returned that same affection to you. Until you have been accepted by a feral cat, especially after waiting as you did, the experience is unlike any other feline/owner relationship. That love will only grow and mature with the kittens throughout their lives. The bond you share with them is also quite different than one shared with a tame domestic kitten. This is your well earned gift for the hard work you did in waiting for the kittens to accept you.

For Shadow to roll onto his back demonstrates his total trust and devotion to you. A cat's stomach is his most vital area to keep hidden and protected. A cat will only expose this area of himself when he knows he is loved and in a safe environment. When you look into the eyes of these kittens I'm sure you have noticed the change from fear to affection. With my own feral kitten, although it took much longer, I was truly touched to see the fear in her eyes change to one of peace and contentment.

Always, Jasmine

*Claire's Reply – October 14<sup>th</sup>...*

Remember me? I gave a home to two feral kittens called Shadow and Heidi, and trained them on your advice to love us. Well they progressed really well and both became very affectionate.

I just thought I would let you know that sadly, the little boy tragically got knocked down by a car the other week. I was leaving for work and found him lying on the side of the road. He was only ten months old.

Although we live on a quiet road, he had jumped the wall at the back and managed to get onto a busier road. We are both very upset, naturally, and his sister is mourning the loss of her more timid brother.

We worked very hard to bring him to the affectionate young cat he was, and will remember him that way.

Now we will give as much love as we can to his sister and hope that in time, she will start to be the lively little cat she was before this happened.

Claire

*Jasmine's Reply – October 16$^{th}$...*

I am so deeply saddened by the loss of your Shadow. It seems hard to believe that such a young soul can complete all his work on earth in such a short period of time.

He did though because you will never forget him. As a kitten he worked so hard to maintain his feral nature. However your unconditional love helped him overcome his natural fear.

I experienced this same sadness with a fearful purebred that I purchased many years ago. She refused to bond with me no matter how hard I attempted to win her affections. It took about eight months before she permitted me to hold her but then finally she gave me all of her heart. I had purchased her as a playmate for Caterina my Seal Point Himalayan. Once I had bonded with Candace, my fearful purebred, Caterina became jealous. Although they had a tight feline relationship, Caterina did not like to share her mother's affections.

When Candace was seven months old I found her body by the side of our road much as you discovered Shadow. She had gotten out somehow during the night and was not accustomed to being outside. I was heartbroken but even more so it was difficult to watch Caterina grieve her loss.

I would like to give you advice regarding Heidi as she is grieving and coping without her brother. My Caterina stayed in her cat bed for almost two weeks while she grieved her companion. Although she would acknowledge me she really seemed to prefer her own company. I know you are mourning the loss of Shadow and as you've indicated Heidi has changed with the loss of her brother as well. Nurture yourself at this time because Shadow was a special boy and you are bound to miss his presence in your home. Heidi will eventually adjust to her loss but it may take a few weeks for her to accept the changes in her environment. She is not only mourning her brother but is absorbing the energy of your loss as well.

If you have not read "The Rainbow Bridge" this would be a good time to read it on our web site.

You will be in my thoughts, Claire, as mourning the loss of a cat is always so difficult.

Always,
Jasmine


*Blessed are those who love cats,*
*for they shall never be lonely.*
**- Anonymous**

# The Mysterious Miss Kitty
## - by Jasmine Kinnear

*She clawed her way into my heart and wouldn't let go.*
**- Missy Altijd**

I am well known for loving cats, all cats, and proudly hold the title of official cat sitter for many of my closest friends and neighbours. Lately that intimate circle has grown to include a select number of friends with cat loving acquaintances. I consider this to be more of a joy than an obligation as it has evolved into a valuable learning resource for my writing. It's my greatest pleasure to both be caring for and developing loving relationships with many felines other than my own precious three.

Where else would I be given such a golden opportunity to study and enjoy a variety of beautiful felines peacefully living in their own homes? Every cat I have been privileged to know has not only increased my knowledge but continues to pique my interest surrounding the mystique of felines.

My introduction to Miss Kitty began when my name was passed through a close friend to a professional couple residing with a multi-cat family. Due to their hectic business, both travelled and required assistance for approximately ten days a month when neither would be home. They required a trustworthy cat lover for whom availability at a moment's notice would not prove a problem. Over the years I've acquired an expertise in the study of felines and enjoy my work as a self-employed writer. With a home-based business I was pursued as the perfect candidate for a houseful of felines requiring special care. One of my greatest joys remains discovering the hidden idiosyncrasies of cats and how they are affected by their home environment. I further welcome escaping the monotony of endless writing projects and the responsibilities of my home office.

Emma and Jim resided with a diverse and eccentric multi-cat family. They rented a neglected older house that was conveniently located close to my home. Emma was the true cat fancier and in our initial meeting we spent the morning sharing our common obsession of living with many felines.

While in their home I was first introduced to the newest member of the clan, a tabby feral stray they affectionately named Miss Kitty. Although I was warned of her moody nature, that morning she was particularly affectionate and welcoming to me. Due to her random bouts of abrasiveness, it took several years before Miss Kitty had been accepted by their five other cats. Whereas the other felines were strictly indoor cats, Miss Kitty was given outside access at free will.

The behaviour of feral cats has always fascinated me. I therefore encouraged Emma to tell me as much about her experiences with Miss Kitty as she could remember. She appeared pleased with my interest and was therefore particularly detailed in describing the queen's unexpected arrival. Several years before, the tabby female had made her initial appearance at their back patio door. She didn't appear to be lost but Emma assumed the cat was feral, and due to the cooler fall season probably cold and hungry as well. Miss Kitty, as she came to be known, would only accept food once she was left alone. She would gratefully eat her dinner from behind the security of the patio door once Emma closed the curtains providing her with privacy.

Emma continued to serve Miss Kitty's favourite dinner during the winter months whenever the feral cat made one of her random appearances. The tabby remained a mystery as she would routinely disappear for weeks at a time, and then suddenly reappear at the patio door requesting attention. After a year of coaxing, the cat's trust grew to a degree whereby Emma could remain outside gently speaking to the feline while she enjoyed her dinner.

Eventually Miss Kitty permitted her benefactor closer contact and would vocalize her appreciation when dinner had been served. With dedicated patience Emma eventually tamed the older feral cat into accepting her physical touch. Once gaining the feline's confidence, Emma decided that the cat was now her welcomed responsibility. Miss Kitty had found her place in the world and regardless of her idiosyncratic nature held a special place in Emma's heart.

Miss Kitty was soon taken for an examination which involved a vaccination regime complete with expensive blood work. Before the cat could be exposed to the comforts of her new home it was mandatory to protect the other cats from viral infections. The vet informed Emma that she had indeed rescued a spayed female approximately four years old. Emma confessed that due to her physical appearance she had believed Miss Kitty to have been a much older cat. I mentioned that the life of a stray is difficult and therefore she only appeared more mature due to the hardships of surviving a feral lifestyle.

Emma's devotion for a cantankerous stray who refused all physical contact for months on end absolutely amazed me. Until her vet check, Emma had not even known the cat's sex and the simplistic name of Miss Kitty had originally been offered as an endearment. However the feral had responded to the name and regardless of its gender suitability the name had appropriately stuck.

Emma further displayed acute instincts in comprehending the emotional needs of each of her domestic cats. She began describing their arrival into her home and eccentric personalities in the greatest of detail. I was cautioned however, that I'd probably never see any of them and would be fortunate if I happened to even catch a glimpse of one while visiting. This was a disappointment as I was accustomed to an enthusiastic greeting whenever I was cat sitting. It was my preference to always spend some quiet time to personally bond with each cat in my care. If Emma was correct, then this unkempt home consisting of many feline souls in hiding would indeed be a new and personal challenge.

As the months passed, Emma's prediction proved to be correct as I was never provided with an opportunity to meet any of her indoor cats. On occasion I would catch a glimpse of the odd cat when first entering the house. I could never entice the migrating feline's company as he would hastily beat a quick retreat up the stairs where he'd permanently remain out of sight. However Miss Kitty was a different story for she would be waiting for me as soon as my car approached the driveway. We would share a warm exchange on the doorstep and then enter the house together. It was always at this point that she would diligently mark my legs with her facial scent glands, accepting me as a welcomed presence in her home. A few times I almost tripped as she intertwined herself between my legs as we made our way to her kitchen.

At least once a month after returning from a business trip Emma and I would meet for coffee. I believe she was intrigued with the nature of my work and I was interested in learning more about Miss Kitty. From the first day of our meeting this sweet queen had enchanted me. The longer I was in her company, the more determined I was to capture the essence of her character in my writing. I'd also never experienced a home where the family cats remained hidden, permanently distancing themselves from visiting company. Many felines will eventually migrate to view visitors from a safe distance however Emma's five cats were like spectres in the house.

As a Feline Behaviour Consultant, Emma wanted my professional opinion regarding her extended cat family. In the beginning I was hesitant to comment as I was still reflecting on her felines' unusual behaviour. Not in my practice nor in any other home had I observed such a situation where the felines lived in total seclusion. It was my experience that even the most timid cat would seek my company when their owner was absent from the house. I needed time for reflection and to see Emma and Jim together before passing judgment or providing an assessment. I sensed the felines' distant behaviour may be indicative of some marital disharmony occurring between this couple. When a marriage is unsettled, felines will often react to the scattered energy flowing between a husband and wife. Their preference for isolation in the limited territory of a remote bedroom was alarming and highly unusual. My only contact with 'The Secluded Five' involved cleaning their litter boxes and filling food and water dishes. Once I had left the house, the cats would migrate downstairs to sample the wet food I'd left in the kitchen. However, only the temporary presence of wet food was an effective lure in motivating them to leave their bedroom sanctuary. The dry cat food left outside their room would always be consumed, whereas the downstairs kitchen bowl was barely touched. Even though the house was empty, it was made perfectly clear that 'The Secluded Five' preferred little human contact until Emma and Jim returned home.

Miss Kitty though, welcomed attention and was loudly vocal in appreciation for my company and especially for being served her dinner. Formerly, she may have been a stray but now she was a highly entertaining personality and not in the least bit timid. After spending months privately enjoying this sweet queen's company, I was comfortable providing a profile of her prior life to Emma. I concluded that Miss Kitty had once been a family's beloved Sociable Independent[1]. She had obviously been lost for some reason known only to her and had never found her way back home. In order to survive, she had reverted to a feral lifestyle and was forced to live an extended period of time with little human contact. Fortunately her responsible family had spayed and vaccinated her which kept her from harm once she became lost. She was a smart girl and over time had survived by developing into a skilled and efficient hunter. Therefore she was probably not drawn to their back door as a starving feline simply wanting food. I believe she returned to them on a regular basis due to Emma's warmth and affection. The food was greatly appreciated and naturally accepted by Miss Kitty with gratitude. With time and patience, Emma's sensitivity was able to draw the true nature of this feline back to a domesticated version of her former self.

Although I enjoyed our cat chats I found Emma's cluttered house to have an oppressive atmosphere. Just as with the upstairs 'Secluded Five,' this lovely compassionate woman appeared to also be secluding herself emotionally. Perhaps that explained the dis-ease in the environment and quite possibly

---

[1] Sociable Independent: One of the Felines by Design personalities identified by Jasmine Kinnear in *How to Hide Your Cat From the Landlord*

Emma's unusual patience and irresistible need to tame Miss Kitty.

Emma was in her late 30's, had pleasant features and was full figured giving her an appearance of being very maternal. She had remained childless but never mentioned if this had been by choice. During our coffee get togethers she would initially appear ill at ease. However following the first hour as we continued discussing her cats, she would eventually become comfortable and the conversation became less strained. Even after knowing her for some time the same scenario would take place each time we met for coffee. I accepted that Emma was emphatically kind but simply a shy person by nature. Conversation with her didn't always flow in a natural rhythm as is the accepted norm when two women meet to enjoy each other's company.

On one of our scheduled meetings for coffee sharing and feline exchanging, I was surprised to be met by Emma's husband at the front door. Although I had met Jim several times before it had amounted to only a few moments when he briefly spoke of his business. This time he planned to stay and speak with me until his wife returned from running messages... and speak he did.

Jim was a good natured rather large and heavyset man in his mid 40's. Following business hours his personal time was consumed with an interest in deep sea fishing. In a rare moment of intimacy Emma had surprised me by confessing that Jim had previously been married. Her statement was inappropriately blurted out and really not reflective of our immediate conversation. An intimate exchange between women can be a wonderful experience but only when the conversation merits such a confidence. When women have enjoyed a long and intimate friendship there is no rhyme nor reason to the flow of a conversation. Our discussion did not reflect such circumstances nor the nature of my present relationship with Emma. I was unaccustomed to sharing such a personal confidence with her and therefore remained silent, uncertain of an appropriate response.

Lonely women with few close friends often have a difficult time sharing the private circumstances of their lives. Quite often their timing within a conversation will be wrong and their words may appear inappropriate and awkward. They sense genuine warmth from an acquaintance but are not accustomed to voicing those personal details that concern them. Women by nature will instinctively respond to an unexpected emotional statement from a close friend. As women we are born with an innate understanding of the rhythm and flow of an intimate exchange. Unfortunately, due to Emma's quiet nature she seemed uncomfortable and did not have an instinctive awareness of this concept. I knew she was a compassionate woman and it had been difficult for her to confide in me, however her statement had been ill-timed. Although we only shared a mutual love of cats there was no true intimacy between us. However Emma had now provided an important detail in understanding 'The Secluded Five' who hid in her bedroom.

As I took a seat in the living room, Jim carried in a tray holding a pot of coffee with several mugs. Although he possessed a genuine kindness, Jim would never be considered a handsome man. His face displayed character lines sculpted by the elements earned from his many years spent fishing at sea. I had a passing thought that he wouldn't have approved of my extended knowledge of his personal background nor marital history. However now aware of such information including other snippets from Emma, I had a more accurate impression of him and their feline family. As he began speaking, he initially appeared more comfortable with the art of conversation than his wife had ever been. It was my observation though that Jim enjoyed any conversation as long as he was the one speaking. After finishing everything he had to say on a subject of his own interest, the conversation was abruptly ended and he excused himself from the room.

By the time Emma returned I had a better perception of why Jim and Emma were married and still together. Jim shared the same trait of shyness as his wife however he also loved the sound of his own voice. It was Emma's nature to be a listener however I doubted Jim ever returned the compliment by being attentive to her needs. While Emma joined me in the living room, Jim soon departed for an overnight fishing expedition aboard his treasured old boat.

After spending time with both of them, I believed that this couple dearly loved their cats but there was a lack of true intimacy between them. They shared a need for privacy, but according to Emma did not partake in long conversations even when they were alone. However the love they mutually expressed for their cats was touching and sincere. Jim was a hard working, reserved man with limited interests and gave the impression of being slightly self-absorbed. Emma's shyness prevented her from seldom engaging in any topics other than her beloved cats. Everything else appeared to be too personal to discuss and therefore our conversations were usually severely limited. Every now and then however, she would catch me off guard with a statement such as the one regarding her husband's first marriage. There were several times when she made inquiries regarding the mutual friend who had originally introduced us. However I preferred to keep that subject to a minimum to respect his privacy, managing to avoid a response to any of those questions.

I sensed a deep longing in Emma for companionship. This need though was only being realized in the time she shared with her cats. I was in the house everyday for at least one week each month. During an entire year I only encountered two members of 'The Secluded Five' who by chance were downstairs when I entered the house. Whenever an impromptu meeting may have occurred, the cat would revert into a feral state of flight and desperately panic fleeing to the safety of the upstairs bedroom. This is a bizarre reaction from cats accustomed to the same person responsible for feeding them and entering their home on a daily basis. Miss Kitty was the only affectionate cat in the home and I spent my time thoroughly enjoying her company. There was an air of intrigue and mystery within the house. This may have explained why Miss Kitty preferred to spend most of her time outside awaiting my arrival. The cats were very much like the couple, distant, wary and always on guard. I can usually communicate with all felines on some level however 'The Secluded Five' never welcomed any interaction I tentatively put forth. The cats in this neglected and cluttered house were coping with unknown issues that appeared to vary in intensity on a weekly basis.

Emma soon realized that my affection for Miss Kitty was sincere. She was also aware of my difficulty in assessing the personalities of the seldom seen 'Secluded Five.' As time passed, Emma sought answers regarding the less than favourable aspects of my favourite queen's personality. Recently Miss Kitty had developed a new pattern of awakening the entire household in the dead of night with loud protests of feline wailing. Emma always awoke in a panic, anxious to quiet Miss Kitty's torturous cries before they bothered Jim. She wasn't troubled with having to let the cat out during the middle of the night, but was disturbed with the old girl's escalating cries and physical anger directed towards her. All the way down the stairs and right to the patio door, Miss Kitty would continue to loudly hiss, spit and growl at her mistress. Emma found herself rushing in a panic to open the locked patio door while Miss Kitty would bat and scratch her legs in a state of desperation to get outside. The other five cats were content with several litter boxes however this apparently did not suit Miss Kitty.

What was the problem with Miss Kitty not using the many litter boxes which were available in multiple rooms throughout the house?  Emma confessed that these random nightly rituals with Miss Kitty upset her to such a degree that she often was unable to get back to sleep.  It was my belief that Emma was troubled because she'd associated her cat's anger as a personal rejection of her affections.

I was aware that cleaning litter boxes had never been a high priority for Emma.  'The Secluded Five' however had been raised within the home and had always tolerated their haphazard maintenance.  Not wishing to point out the obvious, I informed her of an accepted fact with felines sharing Miss Kitty's background.   Feral cats are well known for their cleanliness and under normal circumstances will appropriately use a privately concealed litter box.  I told Emma that Miss Kitty may simply prefer not to use the same box as the other cats.  Due to her time as a feral cat she became accustomed to using the outside environment.  Now, despite the convenience of assorted litter boxes being provided she obstinately refused to co-operate.  She insisted on being outdoors to personally select her own area every time the need necessitated.

An explanation for her abrupt manner with Emma was due to her age and being unable to hold her urine for an extended period of time.  Miss Kitty was easily frustrated as a result of all the time and trouble she encountered to awaken her mistress.  For a feline accustomed to the quick convenience of outdoor elimination, she was displaying little patience with the prolonged procedure.  From her perspective she had a great deal of work to do whenever she needed to simply relieve herself late at night.  Emma was amused once having a better understanding of Miss Kitty's midnight temper tantrums.  However this wasn't to be the last area of contention between them.  A few weeks later I was once again consulted regarding two interesting situations involving this queen.  Emma was deeply concerned and sought my advice as she needed to understand the feral queen's perspective.

Emma was a woman possessing a rare instinctive awareness of her many cats. Her emotional attachment appeared to be quite similar to my own and her felines responded in kind. Therefore without the blessings of children to nourish her spirit, the cats filled that need and became her highest priority. Although I have a wonderful son, he is now becoming a young man and doesn't require me in the same manner as when he was younger. Therefore I related with Emma and would empathize when she became easily upset with problems occurring within her cat family that held no explanation.

I took this opportunity to share notes with her from *The Feline Soul Mate Mystique*, a book which I eventually plan to have published. Although it was a personal reflection of my own situation, I knew that Emma had the sensitivity to understand the message behind my work. I had been born into a dysfunctional family and over the last year Emma and I had shared our similar experiences. The mutual connection of treasuring our cats with such an absolute compassion was not as uncommon as may be originally thought by others. I explained to Emma that the relationship she shared with each one of her cats was satisfying an area of her life that was currently being unfulfilled or had been neglected when she was a child. Her cats were her loving companions and often the only ones who shared her emotional highs and lows accepting her unconditionally. Felines, as non-judgmental companions, provide balance and satisfy those emotional needs often lacking within their owners' life. This included Emma's most significant relationships both in unresolved ghosts from her past or unspoken issues within her present circle of confidants.

Emma agreed with me as it appeared to mirror her current situation both at work and at home. When the professional need necessitated, she was able to adapt and become socially inclined, however she preferred isolation and guarded her time alone. I confided in her that although I had treasured friendships, I didn't see them as often as they desired.

Eventually my close friends accepted that I also had the same need to guard my privacy.

Emma commented that she didn't mind Jim's desire to be alone on his boat because it was during this time that she enjoyed some privacy with her cats. She preferred her time alone with them rather than listening to her husband's complaints or current business prospects. She agreed that the time spent away from home for work consisted of the same pattern as had once been my own. She drove endless hours for work and would sleep from exhaustion to begin the very same cycle the next day. Only by de-stressing alone with her cats was she able to maintain the discipline needed to function. Emma felt consumed by a life consisting of endless hours of work and travelling for business.

Every woman's personal situation is unique and will vary. However I have long been an advocate of the notion *rather be alone than wish you were alone.* I shared this philosophy and other confidences of my life with Emma, confiding details that I'd trusted with few of my friends. I understood the peace she sought within her multi-cat family as I had shared the same with my own. Years earlier, after suffering within an abusive marriage of tolerance, the pleasure of my beloved cats for company was truly a sanctuary. Now my life was totally different and although my cats were still one of my highest priorities, my second marriage was a totally satisfying experience.

Emma prompted me regarding 'The Secluded Five' as she'd always been concerned with their preference for isolation in the bedroom. She had originally discovered the abandoned litter by the roadside prior to meeting her husband. It had taken a full month of bottle feeding them and her diligent care to save the litter. Emma sadly admitted that once she married Jim, the cats would only venture from the room when she was alone in the house. At night when Jim was sleeping they would lie with her on the bed as she watched television. Jim had tried to bond with the litter but his affections were rarely returned, with the exception of one gentle female. She would always sit with him when he was in the room and he appeared satisfied with her attention.

I explained that Emma's loving care for the abandoned litter was a time consuming chore not many others would have undertaken. When a feral litter has been hand raised, the kittens will uniquely bond and connect themselves to their new human mother. They will mirror her personality traits in a manner unlike other felines that experienced a traditional rearing with a feline mother. I inquired if the master bedroom was also the place where Emma too sought refuge. When Jim was home she preferred to stay in the bedroom with her cats, reading or watching television. Jim was a sports fan and she was constantly irritated by his preference in television viewing so she usually remained upstairs. Her cats were in essence duplicating her habits and as ferals were also sensitive to the same loud programs that were Jim's preference. The bedroom was therefore the only place they felt safe and the only area where they had Emma to themselves. It may appear as unusual behaviour but now that I'd been made aware of their background and Emma's role in their survival, the bedroom as their preferred territory should not be changed.

*I cannot exist without a cat...*
*Life would not be worth living without a cat.*
**- Peggy Bacon**

Emma appeared satisfied with my assessment and relieved that she wasn't responsible for their voluntary confinement. She had always loved them and accepted their odd behaviour unconditionally. It was only her family and friends who made snide comments regarding her strange cats that she found so disturbing. I replied that without her intervention they would have all died. Tamed ferals, especially an entire litter, should not be expected to behave as other domestic cats. In their manner of relating to her they were exhibiting normal feline behaviour and that was all that mattered. To Emma's credit their survival had been hard work and the litter only survived due to her loving devotion. Her litter of ferals had formed a lifetime bond with her and she had been accepted as their mother. She would more than likely remain the only human they would ever be comfortable trusting.

Miss Kitty had also experienced the difficulties of a feral lifestyle. However despite attempting a warmer relationship, this queen maintained firm boundaries with her loving mistress. Emma remained at her wit's end regarding Miss Kitty's misadventures and explained that Jim simply didn't understand his wife's dedication to the old girl.

Earlier that month Miss Kitty had returned to the house after surviving a vicious backyard cat fight. She had dragged herself home after being severely hurt and collapsed by the back door during the night. Emma had spent a small fortune to ensure that her tough little girl would survive. She hadn't listened to her vet's advice and insisted that her cat's life be saved. It had taken a small fortune, however after several operations Emma paid the high price to save a queen she wasn't even sure loved her. Despite her reserved nature, Emma had been holding back a well of emotion and began crying. She sadly confessed that she didn't believe the cat would ever show her the same affection as Miss Kitty did with me.

All I could tell Emma was how highly I respected her because she placed so much value on the feral's life. I also confessed that it was more a case of cupboard love as Miss Kitty only associated me with her daily dinner. On Emma's business trips I became the visiting Aunty and would spoil her as she was the only cat that wanted my company. Conversely, Miss Kitty had to share her Mom with the other five cats in her home. It was a common dilemma in multi-cat families as each cat sought to be the favoured feline with their mother.

Although Emma didn't appear convinced, she was grateful to know that my relationship with Miss Kitty did not parallel her own.

After that time, while I was in the house I would constantly be speaking to the tabby queen telling her to be more affectionate with her mistress. Without Emma's love, Miss Kitty would not have a home to return to after enjoying a night on the prowl. I would remind Emma that without her care this idiosyncratic queen would have experienced a truly difficult life and probably wouldn't be alive today. In many ways Emma's relationship with her moody queen reflected particulars from her own birth family. Emma never shared a warm relationship with her own mother who had died several years earlier. I had also met Emma's younger sister Sue, who gave an impression that she believed my work with felines was rather ridiculous. She remarked that she didn't care for Emma's rented house, and that statement equally embarrassed her sister. Sue was also the thinner, more glamorous sister and had been blessed with several children. Married and living a more prosperous lifestyle she appeared to be a little self-centered. It was difficult to believe that these two women were sisters raised within the same family.

This meeting confirmed my initial impression that Emma's attraction to the tabby feral was similar to the relationships she shared within her own family. Emma was a pleaser and presented a loving and mothering presence in her home, whereas her sister appeared to be the very opposite. It was obvious from the short time I shared with Sue that all was not well between them. Emma confessed that her physician had warned her to lose weight as she was now subject to contracting diabetes just as her mother had before her. Regarding weight issues, over the years Sue had always been unsympathetic. She was a naturally thin person and had never understood Emma's fluctuating weight problems. Sue's lack of compassion included Emma caring for her many odd cats and their subsequent expenses she could ill afford.

Although I was only in Sue's company for a short period of time, I had a better understanding of why Emma sought to make every soul in her home feel wanted. The year before, Jim's less than pleasant mother had died within a few months of Emma losing her father. Coping with such extended loss and grief left Emma with an even smaller family. Jim had been an only child and her relationship with Sue as an only sister was less than a satisfying experience. The comfortable relationship Emma shared with her cats was now developing an even greater importance. Loving a feral queen that only displayed random episodes of affection was also familiar to Emma. It made greater sense now why rejection from Miss Kitty upset her so much. That rejection mirrored the flawed relationships she had known with both her own mother and her mother-in-law.

By the time Emma and I shared this crucially personal information I'd been caring for her cats for several years. Emma was now aware that her response to Miss Kitty's behaviour reflected childhood issues with her deceased mother. I gently explained that 'The Secluded Five' represented several unspoken issues she had with her husband Jim. Cats can be like sponges, they soak up our emotional conflicts and Emma's were deeply buried... as deeply and physically buried as 'The Secluded Five.' This was reflected in their preference to hide within their safe but limited bedroom space. Emma appeared grateful for my insight once she understood that the cats were reflecting her own fear of life. Miss Kitty however, had a totally different personality and perspective of her world. I explained that Emma had not raised her from a kitten and a feline's personality is formed during their first two years. However the feral tabby queen was well aware that it was Emma who loved her and had saved her life. That remained the mystery… where had Miss Kitty lived before appearing at the back patio door four years earlier?

When Jim's cousin from Scotland arrived for a holiday I was given a break from caring for the cats.  Emma asked that I visit a few weeks after Angus returned home because she was anxious to share an interesting Miss Kitty episode.  No one had ever been able to pick up the feral cat with the exception of Emma on those rare occasions when requiring a veterinarian.  Emma said that when Angus had been alone with Miss Kitty she literally became his shadow.  When he watched television Miss Kitty would sleep on his lap and this was something that had never occurred before.  Although Emma tried to entice the queen once receiving this information, Miss Kitty typically ignored her.  Why… why so many questions and so few answers regarding this precocious tabby girl?

Six months later I was there when Miss Kitty offered several possible answers.  I was invited to a barbecue to meet Angus' parents who were staying with Emma and Jim while on holiday from Scotland.  My family is also Scottish and meeting this couple was a rare treat for me.  Listening to the lovely brogue and watching the affections between the couple was a heart warming experience.  Miss Kitty was right in the middle of the socializing, sitting right between the couple, taking turns lying on one Scottish lap after another.

I was watching Emma's face because as wonderful as it was to see Miss Kitty's affectionate nature, I knew Emma had never received such loving attention from her.   When we spoke several days later I confirmed that Miss Kitty had never sat in my lap either.  I'd also never intimately held her in a manner such as Jim's Aunt and Uncle had for the entire day.  After giving it some careful thought I believed I finally had an answer.  I understood why Miss Kitty had never discarded her fear or her wall of indifference to either Emma or myself.

My grandmother was born in Dundee, and listening to the wonderful brogue and familiar gestures of this loving couple from Scotland had warmed my childhood memories. I felt myself drawn to their company and was greatly comforted by listening to the same thick Scottish brogue as had been my own dear grandmother's. It all made sense now and as I sat with Emma, I watched her eyes well up with tears of compassion as Miss Kitty finally shared her past with us. My explanation was that Miss Kitty had been owned by a Scottish family approximately the same age as Jim's Aunt and Uncle. We live in a city that is proud of our British heritage and famous for attracting English families to retire on our beautiful island. I believe Miss Kitty had probably been lost by chance and never found her way back home, at least not until now.

The most interesting facet of this cat's unique personality is that she would permit no one to pick her up with the exception of the Scottish family that visited yearly. Emma was shocked when Miss Kitty curled up on the adult son's lap, as in several years she had approached neither of them in the same manner. It simply made sense to me that Miss Kitty recognized a more familiar body language and karma from this family. Miss Kitty had been owned by a Scottish family on the island and remembered the essence of her former home. Just as the Scottish family touched my heart and brought back memories of my own family to me, so had the same occurred for the lost tabby queen. Only twice had Miss Kitty ever permitted such intimacies with people, and each time it was with visiting Scottish relatives.

Emma and Jim moved six months after we'd solved the feline mysteries within their house. It has now been several years since I've seen Miss Kitty and apparently she has mellowed with age. I shared with Emma the same passion for felines and also have dealt with severe setbacks in my life. I understood Emma's need for solitary moments with her felines, as during my life there were times when I also needed my own cats to renew my spirit. The last time Emma and I were together we shared both laughter and tears as we reminisced of our collective feline experiences.   As Jim and Emma were moving a great distance from the city I knew our contact would be limited to e-mail only.   I sensed there was a great anticipation within her as they shed the oppressive atmosphere of the rented house.  Having experienced many losses during the years she'd lived there, she had now been provided with answers to many long standing questions.

I was deeply touched by the unselfish nature of this couple by truly accepting Miss Kitty exactly as she presented herself. Apparently in many cats dwells the necessity to facilitate their buried feral nature when their very existence depends on it. I've told Emma that she will be blessed throughout her life for extending such kindness to those tiny feral kittens requiring assistance by the roadside and to Miss Kitty at her patio door. In the last e-mail received from Emma, she said I must have been right because against all odds she'd been given the one and only blessing she'd ever truly wanted. After many years of trying she was finally pregnant with her first child.

*The purity of a person's heart*
*can be quickly measured by how he or she regards cats.*
**- Anonymous**

# The Garden Ferals
## - by Jasmine Kinnear

*He liked companionship, but he wouldn't be petted, or fussed over,*
*or sit in anyone's lap a moment; he always extricated himself from*
*such familiarity with dignity and with no show of temper.*
*If there was any petting to be done, however, he chose to do it.*
*Often he would sit looking at me, and then, moved by a delicate*
*affection, come and pull at my coat and sleeve until he could touch*
*my face with his nose, and then go away contented.*
- Charles Dudley Warner

When this story of adopted ferals was first brought to my attention I became anxious to contact Sam and Dee, a very special couple living in Northamptonshire, England. I needed to hear for myself the entire story of a loving, married couple who rescued an abandoned young queen caring for her feral litter.

This story held significant importance to me for several reasons. As a cat lover I was deeply touched by the devotion of this couple who was providing unconditional love for a mother and her feral litter. As a Feline Behaviour Consultant I was also intrigued by Sam's story of patiently taming the litter by responding to their special needs. Sam and Dee assumed responsibility for catching and neutering the four kittens as well as their mother, Softy. They were willing to share their loving home with the garden ferals, but only if the kittens themselves decided to stay. I believe they were successful due to their never ending patience in meeting each of the feral kittens' specific needs.

This became not only a financial obligation for Sam and Dee, but also gradually developed into an emotionally bonding experience as well. I learned much from my conversation with them and of their unconditional love which they still share with the mother and her litter. Sam and Dee demonstrated an instinctive understanding of ferals with both the mother and kittens responding in kind. As we spoke I knew why the mother reacted to Sam's kindness and why she took a chance by exposing her precious secluded litter to this couple.

In Sam's own words, it was the mother cat he was to eventually name Softy who first appeared:

*"We had a cat many years ago however she died of Feline Leukemia. After several years had passed without owning a cat I hinted to my wife that perhaps we should have another one. I'd also really wanted a dog but by that time we hadn't gotten around to it yet. That's when the mother cat, Softy, appeared at the top of our garden, which stretches about 30*

*yards from the house.*

*She was very frightened. To be honest with you the wife wasn't very keen on having her and kept on shooing her away but Softy always returned. I should imagine it was for a period of a couple of weeks that I'd walk up to the top of the garden to feed her little titbits and so on. Well she just got braver and braver and continued coming back to be fed. At this time however we had no idea that she was also caring for little kittens.*

*A couple of weeks later, after I'd been working nights and sleeping during the day, Dee said to me, 'Come and have a look at something.' She then took me up to the top of the garden and the mother cat was up there waiting for us. However this time she wasn't alone, there were four little noses peering out from underneath the fence. As soon as they saw us however they disappeared like bullets. Over a period of a couple of weeks we managed to tease them through the fence. Eventually they all came and we fed them various bribes of cat food and so on with bits and pieces of ham and what have you. Eventually the mother cat became quite settled and didn't feel the need to run away from us any longer."*

I asked Sam, "While the four little noses were exposed from underneath the fence, was the mother watching and around at that time?"

*"That was eight or nine years ago but I remember, yes, she was half over the fence looking for food and we tested her. The little kittens had obviously followed her, but to a degree they weren't sure. So all we saw were their little noses sticking out from under the fence, peering to see what was going on. Well I think she was trying to bring them to us... because we had fed her and she was quite hungry for obvious reasons.*

*I believe, thinking back, that she was trying to bring them to us because as far as I can ascertain, on the other side of the fence there was a garden that was a bit unkempt. An older woman lived there and she couldn't look after it very well and* to this day I still wonder where they lived in there. There's nowhere for them to be sort of hidden apart from in between a couple of garages, and that's where I am assuming they were born... and so they didn't have very far to come to the fence and crawl underneath. Once we got them used to the fact that there was food they started coming more, and of course, to start with they were ravenous.

I believe the mother must have been someone's cat and the owner had simply thrown her out; whether it was because she was pregnant at that time I know not. Ultimately the other four little cats, they were all very frightened... like feral cats if you know what I mean. Basically that's how they've almost remained as they seem to prefer living outside. They like the top of the garden and their preference is to fend for themselves. Adjacent to our shed there is a lean-to which covers odds and sods of my building days. Within, I've placed a big thick wooden box which I've left on its side. So with the top being open, the top has become the side; inside there is a carpet and they live in there. They snuggle in there... sometimes you can't see one for the other because they are all sort of intertwined sleeping away quite merrily.

When they were kittens they wouldn't let us anywhere near them. They kept on running away, always keeping a safe distance if you will. I did once find all four of them suckling away and the mother calmly lay there. As I quietly approached she could see me, and as she appeared content with me being around she wasn't disturbed. So the four kept suckling and I crept up very slowly and stroked all four of them. They didn't know what was going on. Now looking back I'm sure they had no idea I was there. I could actually stroke all four of them and pull their tails gently and scratch their backs and so on, and they kept on suckling away. The mother cat just looked at me occasionally and laid her head down and continued with the job in hand. After at least five minutes of them being totally oblivious to me, one kitten turned, saw me and bolted with the *other three following behind. That was in the beginning and when they were much younger."*

While Sam was explaining this intimate experience he shared with the kittens I was equally fascinated, marvelling at Softy's intelligence. When a cat has been stroked by their owner, very often they will immediately begin cleaning themselves. Softy wanted her kittens to become familiar with Sam's scent for as he continued stroking each one of the kittens he was, to some extent, masking the babies' personal scent. Sam was placing an overdose of his scent on each kitten. Softy knew they would immediately begin to clean themselves after nursing in an attempt to clean Sam's scent from their fur. Each kitten would then be tasting and reading the signals from the scent of Sam's hands.

As with all good mothers, Softy had practiced allogrooming ever since her kittens were born. She was a loving queen and continued to clean her babies until they were able to groom themselves. This practice is also seen between adult felines in a multi-cat household as a form of expressing their affection for one another. By that time the kittens were over five weeks old and self-grooming, technically known as autogrooming, begins when kittens are approximately three weeks old. Softy was permitting Sam to handle her litter as she had developed a trust in him. She then arranged a situation where Sam would have access to her litter and he followed his instincts by touching her babies. Softy wanted Sam's scent to be incorporated into the personalized family scent of her litter. As the kittens groomed themselves they would be learning to identify Sam as an important extended member of their feline family.

Cat names are extremely important and I'd heard several of the excellent names that Sam had chosen for his five cats. "Softy" is an English expression for someone having a soft heart. Sam's Softy had demonstrated not only her high intelligence but also her ability to care for her kittens under difficult circumstances. According to Sam she was a young cat and he estimated that these babies were possibly her first or second litter. He obviously cared for her welfare and was determined that this litter would also be her last. I mentioned that we don't select a stray cat, the truth being that they select their owner and I believe Softy must have known.

I teased him by saying, "She herself knew a soft touch when she found you. She must have known that you were a softy too." To which he replied, *"Yes, she knew, she knew I was a soft touch, you're right."*

Following his response, I asked him if he knew right away that he wanted to keep them?

*"I wanted them... yeah. I thought it might be a bit of a problem having five of them as Softy's litter included one female and three toms... and Dee didn't want all of them but they grew on her and that was it."*

Left to right: White Paws, Softy and Spot in their garden

I then inquired, "How long did it take you to name them and how did they get their names?"

*"I should imagine about two or three weeks... we didn't*

*know what was going to become of them. We didn't know if they were going to stay or go so we didn't really have names for them as such. However as their characters evolved we had to give them names because we had difficulty recognizing them as they're all black and white. As silly as it might sound now... where we can tell them at a glance... then it was a bit hard. Now their markings are more distinct so even if I have a view of two of them, for example Cheeky and White Paws who are mainly black on their backs, I can tell the difference because of the slight markings. So I suppose it was a few weeks before we came up with the names that we are calling them now."*

"Each one must have done something that made you give them their particular name. Can you recall going back to when they were kittens... how they got their specific names? For example Squeak is an usual name... "

*"Well, Squeak, she continues to make these squeaking noises... "* Sam began.

"So she named herself in other words… and does she still squeak?"

*"Yes, yes, however she no longer lives with us. She's lives over the road."*

"So, Squeak decided she wanted a new home. Do you believe she made the decision to be an only cat?"

*"Well Squeak has an interesting story herself. In the beginning we caught each one of Softy's kittens and had them all neutered, one at a time, with the exception of Squeak who suddenly went missing. Thinking back, she went off and we didn't see her for a long time. I believe Squeak developed quickly and came into season before I was able to catch her. This all occurred quite quickly within several months of Softy arriving with her litter. Although the neutering was a lot of money at the time, I still believe it was money well spent.*

*I'm thinking back to when Squeak first returned; I had been concerned about her while she was missing but when she arrived back home she appeared fine. Within a short period of*

**179**

*time, however, whenever I was in and around the shed I could hear the distinct squeaking of kittens. When Dee or I approached that area they became quiet as they sensed we were there. It actually took me about four or five days to finally locate them. Thinking back I can't recall if there were two or three kittens, but they were squeaking just like their mother. While Dee was preparing food for all the cats and Squeak was also out and about feeding with the rest of the tribe, that's when I finally found her litter. We hadn't been able to catch Squeak to be neutered when we'd caught her brothers and therefore she went off. Fortunately though, she eventually returned home in order to safely have her kittens.*

*Squeak's kittens were born in the same box that I had made for Softy's litter. They were all very small and squeaking just like their mother. Unfortunately they were covered in ticks. It was at that time that I was finally able to catch Squeak and she was quickly neutered. There is a society called the Cat's Protection League in the U.K. and they look after lost cats and so on. Anyway the RSPCA takes care of local concerns all under the general title of the Cat's Protection League. I rang the local ones here and I made a donation to their fund and they took the little kittens off me."*

Squeak had returned not only seeking affection but I believe it was also her need to be with the only family she'd ever known. Once she was pregnant and needed security, she returned to her garden and quietly gave birth in the same box Sam had provided for her as a kitten. Sam discovered Squeak's kittens when they were about three weeks old. When I questioned him regarding the size of the babies he believed he could comfortably hold one in his hand. Although they were small babies, they had inherited their mother's feral nature; according to Sam they remained quiet and hidden from him. Sam has indicated that he could hear the babies but Squeak managed to keep them out of sight.

I believe that Squeak was moving the kittens from time to

time to different areas within the garden in an attempt to protect them from predators. Even purebred felines will also move their babies when born within a safe environment. Queens traditionally are following an innate instinct to protect their litter and despite Squeak's young age, she needed to be near Sam but was cautious with her kittens. Squeak cared for her kittens until they were old enough to leave their mother and were then re-homed by the RSPCA.

I questioned Sam regarding Squeak's new home as she presently lives down the street from her birth family. I was curious why she decided to leave the garden and if she selected the new home of her own volition.

*"I don't know... I don't know why she went across the road when she could have gone in the garden to either side of our house. Personally I think she was driven away by her brothers, with the main culprit for that being Spot. He will continuously drive her away even now. I think if it wasn't for Spot, who does the majority of the chasing, she would probably still be around. The others... she can lie there in the front of the garden and let the others walk past her and she won't even acknowledge them.*

*Spot appears to be the most dominant of all the cats. He tends to be a little bossy and likes to think of himself as our Head Cat but they all play a role in their own little community. Squeak though comes and she visits once a day, generally speaking, to the front of the house where we feed her. However what we tend to do is to feed the other cats first. While they are busy eating, we then give Squeak something if she happens to be there. She eats at the front of the house and will then lie down in the sun and spend a couple of hours there appearing quite content."*

It appeared to me that Squeak was not simply returning for the food that Sam and Dee offered her; I believe she was returning because she trusted Sam and despite her feral nature she sensed how much he cared for her. From everything I've learned during my conversation with Sam he appeared to be a quiet and sincere man. He was not prone to making assumptions, which is why I then asked him, "Why do you think she comes back Sam... Do you think she's coming back to see you?" His simple reply was rather touching; this was a gentleman who was providing unconditional affection for a feline he'd known since shortly after her birth.

*"I don't know. She's still a very frightened and nervous feral cat. I'm not sure whether she's being fed by someone else or if she is finding food. After she had the kittens and we gave her time to recuperate from her operation... almost instantly she left us for the first time. However she kept on coming back occasionally and she was very hungry, so we were feeding her every time she came home. Then she didn't come back for a period of several months and I thought perhaps she'd been run over by a car while crossing the road. However eventually she returned for a little while and then she would disappear again for a few months. The pattern continued, she'd return home and then disappear for another few weeks, so although we always watched for her there was no regularity to her appearances. She would generally be very hungry though when she came back."*

**If the pull of the outside world is strong,**
**there is also a pull towards the human.**
**The cat may disappear on its own errands, but**
**sooner or later, it returns once again for a little while,**
**to greet us with its own type of love.**
**- Lloyd Alexander**

*"I believe Squeak then lived in a garage that belonged to an older couple who weren't using their car and she appeared content there. When these people started using their garage again she then moved on to another house. When I watch her now she goes towards yet another house; whether she lives there I'm not sure because I've not followed her.*

**182**

*We have a routine now where we see her almost every day as she tends to come about five o'clock. She's now fed almost every day so she's generally not starving. However when time has gone by and she's been away for days, weeks and sometimes months at a time, when she does finally return then she is starving. You could see it on her; she would be thin and she would eat ravenously but now she eats only if she hasn't been for two or three days. Sometimes, for example, if I am at work until 7:00 in the evening, she might come but then she'll eventually go before I get home. Should Squeak arrive and remain long enough until Dee arrives home from work then Dee always feeds her. However when I am working other shifts or when I'm off then I'm generally here about four or five p.m. when she appears. I will then feed her as will Dee on weekends when she's home and not working. There are times I'm sure when she comes but we're not here."*

When I asked Sam if he believed that Squeak only came because he was feeding her he replied, *"I think that's the main reason, yes. She will spend some time here but she won't let me touch her. I only stroke her while she is feeding, otherwise she prefers not to be touched. So mainly she's just coming here for the food I think.*

*As five o'clock approaches Squeak generally peers into the front door through the glass window and starts to squeak. When you open the door she squeaks even louder. You can actually hear her from the other side of the house."*

I was curious if Squeak wanted to leave her scent on Sam by rubbing her facial sebaceous scents glands against his legs, however this wasn't her practice. She may not have marked him but sensed that he cared about her because dinner was always promptly served. Sam confided, *"She will let me stroke her while she is feeding but I have to be very gentle. On a couple of occasions she has sort of come to me and rolled over and allowed me to stroke her but she's very, very nervous."*

Following his response I further enquired if when Squeak

rolls over, does she prefer to have him stroke her stomach or her back? He replied that she prefers to have her back stroked. Whereas she had rolled over in his presence only a couple of times, the others did it on a daily basis. I told him that it was one of the highest compliments a feral cat can give their person, that of rolling onto their back and exposing the vulnerability of their stomach area.

I was also curious which one of the cats he considered to be most intelligent. Was it the mother or one of the boys?

*"I think the mother is the smartest,"* was his opinion.

That didn't surprise me because she had so wisely connected to a kind family and understood that both Sam and Dee instinctively cared for her kittens. She also made sure the kittens would eventually bond with the couple, arranging herself in a position whereby Sam could have access to her litter while she was nursing them. Scent exchanging was important for the kittens to be able to identify Sam as a safe family member.

Having lived in a multi-cat family I know felines lobby for a position of hierarchy within their feline community. Sam and Dee lived with five cats from the same family and therefore I was interested in the role each cat had adopted over the years they'd owned them. I questioned him regarding the individual personalities of Softy, the mother, and the three toms, White Paws, Cheeky and Spot.

Sam believed Cheeky was a bit of a clown replying, *"I suppose Cheeky, he's aptly named. Right now he's running around up and down all over the place. Spot tends to be a little on the bossy side as he sits in his garden being quite aloof trying to be the resident Head Cat. As Spot tries to be Head Cat... you'll see occasionally as they walk past one another... one will take a swipe at the other and there will be a little 'tête à tête' stand off until one surrenders. Generally speaking though, Spot is the one who starts these little commotions.*

*The reason cats climb
is so that they can look down on
almost every other animal –
it's also the reason they hate birds.*
**- K.C. Buffington**

Top to bottom:
Cheeky and Spot

I then asked him to explain how Cheeky and White Paws received their names. White Paws is the distinguished tuxedo gentleman that graces the cover of this book. I was initially drawn to how intriguing a cat he appeared to be and knew he was harbouring his own interesting story. I mentioned to Sam, "I love the picture of White Paws on the front cover. I mean the green against his black, he looks so mysterious and yet you can tell that whoever took the picture, it's apparent that he loves them very much. It's obvious by the expression on his face and his body language that he's comfortably studying a trusted family member."

*"You're quite right. Very mysterious he is indeed, he likes to hide in the shade of that particular tree and Dee took the picture. He's quite fond of Dee."*

I replied that whenever I'm looking at pictures of felines, I can always tell when a picture has been taken while the owner

**185**

wasn't in the cat's presence. However when it's the cat's owner taking the picture, then there is an expression on the cat's face that isn't caught in any other pictures. I believe cats immediately react and respond by communicating their perception about everything and everyone in their world. Therefore they tend to be the most cooperative and photogenic when being photographed by their owners. Sam agreed with me and said, *"It's in their eyes, you can tell."*

*"White Paws is a bit like Spot as well. He tends to just sit there and when he has to walk past Spot for any reason, he'll take a sort of detour and... surf and navigate so to speak because he knows that Spot's going to throw a punch. It's only banter though... playful banter because they all stay quite close to home. They know where they are better off. They sometimes wander off at night but the general rule is that if you call them they're always only a garden or two away; they don't tend to roam into other areas. They are also well behaved for the most part unless the odd unknown territorial tom wanders into their garden. Then they join together as a family and have a squabble every now and then with a lot of fur flying. We do have the occasional scuffle outside but not very often."*

**It is in the nature of cats**
**to do a certain amount of unescorted roaming.**
**- Adlai Stevenson**

In every multi-cat family much is learned by the manner in which the cats both eat and sleep, so I asked Sam about the sleeping arrangements of the full grown adult males. He confirmed that they still slept together in the back garden in the old wooden box that he had constructed for them. However I was curious if they all slept together as they had when they were kittens or if they now claimed their own special place where they lay separately but in close proximity to one another.

*"I tend to find Cheeky and Spot huddled together in such a*

*fashion that you can't tell where one finishes and the other begins, they intertwine. White Paws will tend to be just a few feet away not entirely with them, close but not far away.*

*The few times that I have seen them with Softy, their mother, she's not with them directly but in the vicinity. Again, Softy is slightly away from the group of Cheeky and Spot who are always together. Softy, their Mum, will only be a foot away."*

Sam has developed a warm relationship with the mother Softy. Although she likes to sleep with her boys she also enjoys time with Sam. Softy lives up to her name and is the only cat who has a preference for spending time inside the house with Sam and Dee. According to Sam, Softy will permit him to hold her however when he tries to cuddle her she has her own preferences.

*"I try to keep her on my lap but she tends to jump down, her preference is to lie on my feet. She's quite content to lie and snuggle her head on my feet and sleep the evening there. We've had the litter for eight or nine years now so possibly Softy may be ten years old. When she first appeared I believe she was a young cat and this was probably her first, possibly her second litter.*

Softy resting in the house

*We feed them all together and she will go and eat with them but she only has a little bit, she wants to be fed on her own. When we were feeding them in the early days she would always let them eat first. She would eat a certain amount but she always, after a while, would sit back and let them eat... she was a very good mother.*

*As kittens they were all about the same size. The only thing that I can recall is that Cheeky was very ill. He would have violent coughing fits. You know when a cat chokes on something and it was like coughing... he wouldn't choke on anything. He just had these coughing fits and I thought he was going to part this world but he didn't, he survived. I was worried about Cheeky but we couldn't catch them to take them to the vet. It didn't matter what we tried, we couldn't catch them. Eventually though they were caught. They tended to be very quiet in the car on the way to the vet. Cheeky would make a bit of a noise but the rest of them would sit quietly and make no noise at all.*

*After they had been neutered and were brought back home we put them in the kitchen for one evening. That night they settled down into their respective corners and just worried about what had happened to them. The next morning as soon as we opened the door, there you go, out they went... we couldn't keep them in. Now we have it that I can approach most of them and they let you touch them but not always, with cats beings cats. Sometimes they are a bit aloof. When they are sunbathing in the garden they don't want to be touched or bothered. We have our favourites so the wife has Spot, as she calls him, he's always around her feet. Whenever Dee is in the garden he will walk around her feet and want to be petted and have his tummy scratched and he'll roll on the ground."*

I remarked to Sam that Spot appeared to have abandoned much of his feral nature as he had affectionately accepted Dee. Sam agreed but mentioned there was still a bit of feral tendencies in Spot. We then discussed White Paws as he played an important role in the family. Sam is quite fond of White Paws and as he's the cat that graces the front cover of this first volume of *Every Cat Has A Story*, I was interested in White Paws' story.

According to Sam, *"White Paws is a little mysterious. He will sit underneath that tree just as in the picture and just watch you go by. It is one of his favourite places to sit in the garden as he is looking towards the house and observing everything.*

*The tree that he sits underneath, I don't know what you would call it, it's like a fir tree I believe. It's not tall, and around the base of it you will sometimes see all four of them sleeping when the sun shines there. The mother cat and the three tom cats will all line themselves around the base of the tree. As the sun becomes too hot they crawl underneath slightly into the shade and when they cool down they crawl out again, they are continuously moving in and out. We have got a few photographs with all four of them around the tree.*

*White Paws is the only cat with a variety of personal family names that he answers to and we use just between ourselves. It's rather complicated but it's because he has basically a black face and it looks as if he has grown one of those long curved up twisted white moustaches. We tend to call him in a foreign tongue and this is where the problem lies as others can't pronounce it. Our parents hail from the Balkans and for White Paws we use the Balkan phrase for moustache just between ourselves. When we have guests over and they ask what is his name then it's easier to just call him White Paws.*

White Paws
sporting his moustache

189

*We call Softy... Softy... Cheeky is always called Cheeky... Squeak is always called Squeak but White Paws has his own special name that we tend to use amongst ourselves. They all know their individual names and will respond by flicking their tails up... and Cheeky, if I call him he will meow and walk towards me.*

*White Paws... or White Socks... whatever you want to call him, he will come to me and the wife in equal measures, especially at feeding time... and the other one, Cheeky, he will come to me most times. I can see him wandering around the garden now. Cheeky earned his name because he has a cheeky personality and he's marked very well too.*

*They all eat together as a group at the same time, that's fair enough. We also offer them titbits at other times of the day and we try to be fair by giving a little bit to one and a little bit to the other. However if you give Cheeky something to eat, once he's finished he'll then sneak up to the others and with his paw will try and hook it away from them very cheekily... and under their noses quite literally."*

**God made the cat in order to give man the pleasure of caressing the tiger.
- Unknown**

Sam feeding
Cheeky, White Paws, Softy and Spot

**190**

*"I think White Paws demands the main dish and is the biggest eater of the group. He gets in there first, has his fill and can eat for a long time and eat a lot. Spot eats his food very quickly and doesn't tend to have as much. When he's done he bolts quickly but White Paws and Cheeky are the two that will sit there and keep on munching away until it's gone or they can't eat any more."*

Having had a cattery I know how expensive it is to provide nourishing food for many felines so I asked Sam if he had any idea how much he was spending on cat food every month? To which he admitted, *"Not really, I've not worked that out but they eat well and they eat often."*

When I spoke with Dee she admitted that Spot was her favourite. Spot received his name because he has a black spot on his face.

*"His face is nearly white but on one side he has a black mark and we gave him the name Spot so we could distinguish him... so he was named fairly early on."*

Commenting on the obvious affection White Paws is showing on this book's cover, Dee then admitted:

*"Yes, the two of them... they are both my favourites. They do sometimes get jealous of each other... if you stroke one of them and the other one comes along, he doesn't like it at all but they're okay. Normally they are alright as I pay equal attention to both of them."*

This story meant so much more to me because weeks following the interview with Sam and Dee I was still thinking of Softy and her bravery in protecting her young litter. As I worked from my notes to compile the story of Softy and her babies, at times I would find myself in tears. I wasn't too sure why she touched my heart but even after completing a day's work on this story, Softy would stay with me. Eventually I felt compelled to write these words as I felt so connected to this lovely feline who raised her litter under extraordinary circumstances. My love for cats is well known but with this story I was drawn to the tale of a mother protecting her babies in an uncertain world and against great obstacles. My connection to Softy, I realized, was extremely personal as I too had raised my son alone. I'd faced financial obligations and other difficulties due to his special needs with the same dedication as Softy had in caring for her litter. I remember working so hard many days that I would stumble out of the car arriving home after 6:00 p.m., having left the house before dawn. Mark is now a grown man, however those years of buried memories in caring for him were touched by Softy's situation of being lost and alone caring for her litter.

Softy respects the distance that her grown kittens demand but remains close to them. She still mothers them but stays a respectful distance away, observing and respecting them as adult felines. When the interview was over I was left with a strong respect for Softy in trusting such a wonderful family with her litter of feral kittens. They were born in a garden and adopted by a couple who respected their feral nature and truly loved and honoured each kitten. The affection for their multi-cat family was obvious in their voices; I was truly touched and wanted to know so much more. I have such a strong desire to visit the U.K., especially as I have family living there whom I've never met and yet miss so much. I am also hoping that Sam and Dee will permit me the opportunity to meet their beautiful cats. Even if I'm only permitted to see them at play in their garden through the kitchen window.

Cheeky and Spot through the
kitchen window

I have enormous respect for this lovely couple. They have, with compassion and love, provided a home for what may have started as garden ferals but are as beloved and precious as any purebred feline I've ever known. During my interview with Sam it was important that he knew just how deeply I respected what he had accomplished. I told him that I believed his story was very special and that he deserved acknowledgement.

I said, "Sam, what you've done is unusual and very special. Feral cats are unique and they bond with their owners in a manner that's quite different from other cats. I've also owned a feral cat from the time she was only five weeks old. Although she has remained an inside cat, in the beginning she wouldn't permit anyone to even get physically close to her. Ten years old now, she's very affectionate, with her feral memory long since forgotten. It takes much time and patience to own five feral cats who want to be around you. Sam, I believe you and Dee are special people. Well you're a man and you love cats so you must be absolutely wonderful because that does not happen every day. I know the cost and obligation of taking care of so many cats. I remember how expensive it can be, especially their vet care. I believe your five cats sense, on some intuitive feline level, just how much you've done for them and how much you care."

If anyone has earned themselves a place in heaven then I believe that due to their unconditional kindness it would be Sam and Dee; and I'm sure Softy, White Paws, Spot, Cheeky and Squeak would also agree.

A week after I'd completed the first draft of Sam's story I received an e-mail from him. Having enjoyed his message so much I requested his permission to include it with his story. My contact with Sam both by telephone and e-mail has been simply delightful. I decided it would be best to not incorporate his e-mail into the text as it would lose Sam's special charm. Therefore in conclusion I'd prefer to use Sam's own words:

*My tribe of cats are all well and flourishing. The weather here is bad and they are more lethargic than usual. I have checked some old photos and we are fairly sure that the cats have been around for about nine or ten years, so I suppose they are quite old in human terms.*

*Softy is always in the house during the evenings sleeping at our feet due to the inclement weather. Squeak still visits every evening for food and I sometimes see her in the early hours of the morning when I come home from work early from a night shift. She seems to recognise the sound of the car engine. The three tom cats spend most of their time lazing about in the garden or on top of neighbours' shed roofs. Cheeky seems the more active as he is seen to be doing circuits of his terrain more often than the other two. He is more muscular as a result of his frequent travels.*

*White Paws is the fatter of the three toms and he is often seen under the tree as in the photograph. He is generally always the first to appear when titbits are on offer. Spot is the thinnest; he always seems to eat less than the others and always bolts his food. He is also less tolerant of Squeak and when she sees him she runs off immediately. When I admonish him over this he disappears under the tree and will be wary of me for a couple of weeks. The cats all generally get along although sometimes they take a playful swipe at one another. Softy has been seen on a few occasions biting and chasing Cheeky around the garden. He rarely defends himself in these situations. White Paws however fights back with one paw and a standoff occurs. The only time that we have a serious scuffle is when a strange cat appears and one of the toms challenges it. The others will either rush to see what is happening or hide. Sometimes these encounters result in cuts that go septic and we have to tend to them if the cats allow it. White Paws and Spot have had the worst injuries but recover very well from them.*

*Regards, Sam*

194

Left to right: Spot, White Paws and Softy

*Cats seem to go on the principle that
it never does any harm to ask for what you want.*
**- Joseph Wood-Krutch**

195

# A Valentine's Day to Remember
## - by Jasmine Kinnear

*A beating heart and an angel's soul, covered in fur.*
**- Lexie Saige**

Several years ago I received a forwarded e-mail regarding relationships. Not the typical forward one so quickly deletes, this one was special and really touched me. I believe that even our most solid relationships deserve nurturing and should be honoured with respect. Relationships are those fragile and emotional connections that make our lives so worthwhile.

This e-mail was a gentle reminder that not all relationships will be everlasting. Some people will remain for the duration of our lives while others will stay for only a season; and then there will be those precious few who briefly touch our lives for a singular reason.

## <u>Reason, Season and Lifetime</u>
- Brian A. "Drew" Chalker

*People always come into your life for a reason, a season*
*or a lifetime. When you figure out which it is,*
*you know exactly what to do.*

*When someone is in your life for a REASON,*
*it is usually to meet a need you have expressed outwardly or*
*inwardly. They have come to assist you through a difficulty,*
*or to provide you with guidance and support,*
*to aid you physically, emotionally or even spiritually.*
*They may seem like a godsend to you, and they are.*
*They are there for the reason you need them to be.*

*Then, without any wrongdoing on your part or at an*
*inconvenient time, this person will say or do something to*
*bring the relationship to an end.*

*Sometimes they die, sometimes they just walk away.*
*Sometimes they act up or out and force you to take a stand.*
*What we must realize is that our need has been met, our desire*
*fulfilled; their work is done. The prayer you sent up has been*
*answered and it is now time to move on.*

*When people come into your life for a SEASON,*
*it is because your turn has come to share, grow or learn.*
*They may bring you an experience of peace or make you laugh.*
*They may teach you something you have never done.*
*They usually give you an unbelievable amount of joy.*
*Believe it! It is real! But, only for a season.*
*And like Spring turns to Summer and Summer to Fall,*
*the season eventually ends.*

**197**

*LIFETIME relationships teach you a lifetime of lessons;*
*those things you must build upon in order to have a solid*
*emotional foundation. Your job is to accept the lesson, love the*
*person/people (anyway); and put what you have learned*
*to use in all other relationships and areas in your life.*
*It is said that love is blind but friendship is clairvoyant.*
*Thank you for being part of my life.*

I tend to be a pleaser by nature, however I prefer my acts of kindness to be anonymous, preferably even to the recipient themselves. For example, nothing provides me with greater pleasure than to feed an expired downtown meter especially when the city parking authority is standing nearby. Although the vehicle's owner will never know of my good deed, it only matters that my change prevented them from returning to an expensive parking ticket. I've practiced random acts of kindness all my life simply because of the pleasure they afford me.

After breeding Himalayan cats for many years my dedication towards felines became well known in our neighbourhood. So much so that a friend seeking my address stopped her car to inquire where her friend, the cat breeder lived. Directions were quickly provided from an unknown pedestrian and unannounced she arrived on my doorstep from Seattle, Washington. I was rather surprised to see her after virtually no contact for over ten years, however it was her manner of locating my home that was even more unsettling. I had been under the mistaken assumption that my business had gone unnoticed in the area. Therefore it wasn't a comforting thought to realize that my presence had become so well known that even a stranger knew of the "cat breeder's" home. This was all due to an American friend's lapse in memory in neglecting to bring my address with her.

Several years later I closed my cattery and was comfortably residing with a small trio of felines. I turned my attention to writing books, with a passion to educate novice cat breeders in the art of feline behaviour and cattery management. I lived in a multi-cultural area consisting of many expensive Victorian era homes, modern duplexes and several less than desirable welfare apartments. The rich lived beside the poor, with an older tattoo shop being situated right next to an exclusive art studio. The area attracted people living on all levels of the social and economic ladder of life. Personally, as a single mother, I rented a small duplex and considered myself blessed when I still had groceries and my bank account was balanced at month's end.

Janet, a friend and relatively new neighbour would always arrive on my doorstep unannounced for a quick ten minute chat. Although she never mentioned her condition, as time passed I came to the conclusion that she was sadly allergic to my cats, thus the short duration of her many visits. We had originally been introduced by a mutual acquaintance many years before when our sons were toddlers. Recently she had been fortunate to acquire a rental suite rather close to my home. I enjoyed Janet's company despite her slightly eccentric yet equally endearing manner. We shared circumstances which can only be appreciated by struggling single mothers raising sons.

Although she often interrupted my writing, she assumed she was always welcomed. With her distinctive knock on my front door I would reluctantly abandon my current writing project. Despite the shortness of her visits I found her daily routine of disrupting my work a little frustrating. Yet she was an engaging person coping with a 'self-imposed' difficult life. Despite it all, she was optimistic and always wore a ready smile. Her warm personality coupled with her need for my company was a little flattering. She claimed her daily contact with me to be therapeutic as our conversations kept her life in balance. I knew every intimate detail of her life and yet she knew very little of mine as I was always the listener and that remained my preference.

She arrived one morning carrying a great sense of urgency about her. This was not unusual for Janet, however this time her concern centered around a friend. Due to her warm nature and basic kindness she was sincerely worried about a neighbour.

"My friend Vincent, you know the guy who lives next door to me, well he needs some help. The cat he's had for years is sick, well she's really his baby. He's wanted to come over because he's heard of your cat knowledge. But he doesn't know you and he's a little shy. I told him that you were the only one who would have the right advice so do you mind if I give him your telephone number?"

For the last 20 years I have been quietly involved in the Cat Fancy World. I have written for feline publications and have also been awakened in the dead of night due to an owner's concern over a sudden decline in their cat's health. The decision on whether immediate expensive medical attention was necessary or if their cat could wait until regular office hours was often the motivation for the contact. Canadians are polite by nature, and cat loving Canadians even more so. Therefore those midnight telephone calls were only made when the urgency demanded it.

Having bred felines for so many years and having a sincere passion for all cats, domestic to purebreds, I've always tried to make myself available. I've been honoured that many times my name was passed through the mysterious network of cat loving friends... one to another, of my reputation to assist during a cat lover's emergency.

"Not a problem, Janet," I reassured her. "He's welcome to call any time."

Although I was actively pursuing a career that centered around my passion for cats, I was also working physically difficult 70-hour weeks outside the house. Janet was well aware of my hectic working schedule and mentioned that she would caution Vincent of the times that were the most convenient for me.

My working day normally began at 5:00 a.m., however on occasion I was still working at 6:00 p.m. By day's end all I wanted was dinner, a hot bath and then my bed before 7:30 in the evening. Several days following my conversation with Janet I'd finished my working day on schedule and was already in bed when the telephone rang. Due to my hectic work schedule and high level of fatigue, my friends always telephoned early. This call was unexpected.

The conversation with Janet had slipped my mind after several days, and it had taken Vincent time to muster up the courage to contact me. He asked if he could come over right away to discuss his cat's health and promised not to stay long. However he stressed he really wanted my truthful opinion because Penny had been sick for several weeks and there were no signs of improvement. I invited him over right away and reached for my housecoat as fall can be chilly in Victoria. I wanted to be waiting for him on my doorstep because I was concerned about the possible exposure of feline viruses to my own cats.

Vincent arrived a few minutes later and as I had anticipated he was affectionately cradling his domestic girl Penny in his arms. My concern was had I not been waiting outside and he felt tempted to bring her then my own cats would be at risk. As he approached I immediately knew that his queen didn't have much longer to live. We sat together side by side on my front steps and I held Penny on my lap gently stroking her long fur. The lustre of her coat was gone. She was alarmingly small and due to her mature age of 13, I suspected her kidneys were shutting down. After a series of questions, although she demonstrated aspects of kidney failure there was still a possibility of viral infection.

"I would have brought her to the vet," he explained shaking his head sadly, "but six weeks ago I lost my job just about the same time she became ill. I kept on hoping it would go away but she hasn't gotten any better."

Vincent was a young man, slight in build and he calmly spoke in a quiet voice. I knew from the way he handled Penny that she was the only light in his life. I also knew that she didn't have much time left and would be yet another loss for him. Vincent needed to see a vet because Penny was suffering and yet he didn't have the money to pay for a large veterinarian bill.

I explained to him about the importance of Penny receiving veterinarian care as soon as possible. I asked if he could arrange for transportation to a small community about 20 miles from Victoria. He believed he could.

I went back into the house and pulled a small gold purse from my bedroom drawer. For the last five years I had been purchasing my cat food from a veterinarian who issued $2.00 coupons that were to be used for vet care only. Every time I bought a large bag of food I had received one of these coupons, and I was saving them for a rainy day when I wouldn't have the money but would need a vet. That rainy day hadn't happened so far and I had several hundred dollars in coupons saved.

I returned outside to Vincent and handed him all the coupons I had saved over the last five years. I told him to make an appointment and to use these coupons as they should more than cover the cost of her care. My reward at that moment was the look on his face, someone cared and would back their commitment with money. Truthfully, when you exist by living from paycheque to paycheque you develop a respect for how difficult life can be. It leaves an emotional scar on your soul when you need to help a beloved cat and the money simply isn't there.

He thanked me, saying that he didn't know how he was going to repay my kindness. I told him that one day the Universe would present a situation where he'd be in the position to step in and help another. That was all he owed me, that he would lend a hand when someone else's need was presented to him. He nodded in agreement and promised to call regarding the vet's examination. He then left carrying his beloved Penny back home in his arms.

Several weeks later during one of Janet's impromptu visits she told me how much it meant to Vincent that I'd helped him. She said the cat had been put to sleep as she was dying from kidney disease. Vincent had wanted to thank me in person but he was deeply grieving her loss and felt unable to leave his apartment. I personally understood how devastating his loss was, especially when he had appeared so sensitive and frail. I asked Janet to tell him that I understood but for now he should only be concerned with taking care of his own needs.

During that period in my life I felt pulled in many directions. The responsibility of supporting and caring for my son coupled with long hours of work became overwhelming. Somehow I always managed to make ends meet although I was left exhausted. I had been single for over ten years and although it was lonely at times, the emotional and physical abuse from my marriage had left a bad taste in my mouth. *Better be alone than wish you were alone* was Janet's philosophy and although she often failed to follow her own words of advice, I made a vow that I always would.

I spent most of my time in solitary contemplation however I was rarely troubled by the isolation. I not only worked alone, but living with a teenage son meant I was usually alone in the house with only my cats for company. I accepted my life and was grateful for those rare and blessed moments of not working and being left alone in peace and quiet. Nothing pleased me more than surrounding myself in bed with my beloved cats while enjoying a glass of fine wine and watching a favourite movie. Dolores, my life long best friend had once mentioned that I was a person who was easily pleased. Her offhanded remark had bothered me but after careful consideration I realized there was a difference. It wasn't that I was a person so easily pleased but rather I recognized and appreciated the many blessings I had been given during my life.

I knew living in a run down duplex with only cats for company and working at a dead end job didn't appeal to Dolores but I was still full of gratitude. Mark and I had food to eat, the cats were healthy and we had a roof over our heads; albeit it was only a rented roof.

I was visiting with my girlfriend, Dana, one late afternoon and despite many years of marriage she was excited because it was Valentine's Day. She knew her husband had something special planned and was looking forward to their evening together. Dana is a sensitive person and in the middle of enjoying her excitement she made a comment that touched my heart.

"Doesn't it hurt you to be alone on Valentine's Day?"

I was both moved and surprised by her sensitivity. However after living for many years without a significant other, I rarely gave any thought to my situation or the chances of meeting someone.

I replied, "Actually I prefer it this way, Dana. I don't have to take care of a man's expectations. I can go home and love my cats and that's enough for me."

Truth be known, I had long given up on the 'Knight in Shining Armour' rescuing me from a life of endless work and responsibilities. As I drove home I realized how many years had passed since I had wanted anyone in my life. I almost wished that Dana had never posed such a caring question because I knew that with my son working I would once again be entering a cold and dark house.

By the time I was parking the car in front of my duplex, it was dusk with the lights just flickering on across the street.

From the car I noticed that there was a package left on my doorstep including a sleeve of professionally wrapped flowers. I knew it was just another delivery error. I often received parcels for the apartment building next door and I would usually walk over and make the delivery myself.

I approached the front steps to see a card displaying my name on the flowers with other items buried within the small box. Although I searched my memory, there wasn't anyone I knew who would provide such an unexpected surprise for me, especially on this traditional day of sweetheart gift giving.

I entered the house carrying the unexpected treasures. Standing in my kitchen I proceeded to open the small gifts included with the flowers. There was a bottle of wine, scented candles and a box of chocolates. Normally I would have opened the card first however I was rather puzzled. I could only wonder why anyone would offer such a sweet gesture. Finally after a few moments of hesitation I could no longer resist the temptation.

The card was bulky and as I opened it I realized all the veterinarian coupons I'd given Vincent were inside. His words were simple but poignant, bringing tears to my eyes:

> *"Thank you so much for your time and kindness to Penny and me. You were right, she was sick with kidney disease but she's at rest now. Forgive me but I'm still too upset to speak to you however please know that you made a real difference. My friend brought me to the SPCA and as it was a medical condition they didn't charge me for putting her to sleep. I won't ever forget how much you cared... and I will pass on the same kindness to another as I promised... Vincent"*

I only saw Vincent that one evening carrying his beloved Penny in his arms. Although over a decade has passed, I've never forgotten his sensitivity or his kindness on that lonely

Valentine's Day.  In the end I was the one who needed an act of kindness, some Universal message that I wasn't forgotten and that quite possibly there was someone waiting for me in the future.  I can look back now and realize that Vincent gave me the encouragement to continue and that 'Knight in Shining Armour,' well eventually when the time was right he did arrive and he was well worth the long wait.

 I believe that our lives are simply a reflection of our actions including everything we say or do.  Life will give you back  everything you have given to it.  The direction of our lives is not a coincidence, it is truly a reflection of ourselves.

*One of the oldest human needs is having someone to wonder*
*where you are when you don't come home at night.*
**- Margaret Mead**

# Caterina, Portrait of a Feline Soul Mate
## - by Jasmine Kinnear

*Cats are glorious creatures*
*who must on no accounts be underestimated...*
*Their eyes are fathomless depths of cat-world mysteries.*
**- Lesley Anne Ivory**

Before starting my cattery I was trapped in a miserable relationship. Totally exhausted, I was working full time and raising a beloved infant son with hidden special needs. I believe now that the Universe knew the time was right and I needed her.

Even today many years since her passing, I still envision her, Caterina my beloved Feline Soul Mate. She remains a part of me and is an integral part of my writing. She has become the focus of my everlasting quest to assist others in the search for their own special feline. Those with the same passion for cats will instinctively understand and acknowledge if they have owned such a feline. Those yet to experience such a kitten may be pursuing their search with this book having been presented as their guide.

Before the marriage, before my beloved son, it began with the rescuing of a lost Seal Point Himalayan while on a weekend getaway in Qualicum Beach. A beautiful feline had perched herself on the raised ledge of the entrance to our hotel to greet the arriving guests. She was so endearing, originally I thought the hotel had acquired a resident cat and she was simply in her element as the official greeter. During the next 24 hours as my mother and I entered and exited the hotel, it became apparent this gentle female was pursuing far more than a simple greeting. She was lost and actively seeking her owner. This sweet feline with inherited patience from her Persian bloodline, coupled with trust from her Siamese genes was confident in locating her missing owner if she simply maintained her position.

I questioned the front desk regarding her welfare and was informed that she had been in the same place for several days. The following afternoon while the winds built into a horrific rainstorm I couldn't stay warm inside our room while the cat remained outside weathering the elements. I left with a large bath towel in hand only to discover she had abandoned her position by the hotel entrance. Circling the extensive grounds of the hotel I finally located her sheltered between two large bushes. She had positioned herself to remain visible while still actively watching for her lost mistress. Drenched from the rain she permitted me to scoop her up in the towel. Somehow she must have sensed I'd been sent to protect her from the storm.

We entered the hotel from a rear entrance as I knew her presence would not be deemed acceptable by the staff. After an examination in our room she appeared healthy but was obviously starving and suffering terribly from a heavy flea infestation. While my mother kept her company I drove to a pet store for supplies some thirty miles away from the hotel.

It is my belief that pets instinctively know when you are not a threat but are attempting to assist them. Upon my return this little darling endured several flea baths without any struggle. She remained wrapped in a fresh towel to dry and later permitted me to continue drying her heavy coat with my hairdryer. After a nutritious meal she was then content to sleep on a pillow for the remainder of the afternoon.

Although I contacted the local radio station, in my heart I was hoping she would not be claimed. I had planned on returning to the store in the morning for a carrier to transport her back to my home in the city. I was totally captivated by her gentle personality and the colouring of her Seal Point coat. However as much as I wanted her this simply was not meant to be. The radio station telephoned our room early the next morning and we were informed that her frantic owner had been located. An older lady who owned this lovely girl had left her in the temporary care of a neighbour. Miss Touch of Class Tiffany then escaped a few days later and travelled several miles from her home to the hotel. Tiffany assumed her position by the hotel's entrance and anxiously awaited her mistress' return.

Although I was pleased to reunite Miss Tiffany with her mother it also left me with a greater awareness about myself. I knew that somewhere and at some other time I would encounter another Seal Point Himalayan cat who was destined to become my own.

Over the next two years I gave birth to my son, Mark, became a cat less person and endured a marriage of tolerance with an alcoholic husband. Despite these painful learning opportunities the Universe provided for my guidance, I have also discovered that nothing in life remains the same... good or bad.

When Mark was a baby his father would often travel for business which always brought a welcomed relief into our home. During one of his business trips good fortune arrived one afternoon by way of the mail. I received a final unexpected cheque from my last government job. Holiday pay in the amount of exactly $250 was a wonderful surprise and I already knew where the funds were destined to be spent. I had been desiring a cat for a very long time and waited many months anxious for Mark to mature in order that he could comprehend the special needs of a kitten. Mark was 18 months old, an active toddler in love with life and constantly in motion. However he was also gently affectionate with any pets he encountered when visiting our friends' homes. Although uncertain if the time was right for him, I recognized a growing need within myself for the presence of a cat in our home.

There was only one advertisement listed in our local paper for Himalayan kittens. The breeder's ad declared these were "Kittens for Mother's Day." It was the only excuse I needed to place the call.

I inquired if there were any Seal Point females available. The breeder responded that she had one left and was asking $200. I requested she not sell the kitten to anyone else promising to be there within the hour. While Mark napped and my mother came over to care for him I cashed my cheque and proceeded to the breeder's home. Although I acted quickly I don't believe it was a typical case of 'kitten fever'. Had I been told that there were no Seal Point females available I may

210

possibly have hesitated.

In Volume 1 of the Felines by Design Series I detailed my experiences in the first cattery I'd ever encountered five years earlier. A little older now and possibly just a whisker wiser, this time I was going in prepared to match wits with the breeder.

Dianne was living in a larger home than the first cattery I'd seen years earlier. She was far more generous with her time and her cattery appeared clean and professionally organized. On the first level of her home I was brought into a bedroom to meet her last Seal Point Himalayan female. Kittens at twelve weeks of age are quickly outgrowing their irresistible appeal and are in direct competition with the younger babies. This kitten had entered the scruffy coated stage and displayed little interest in acknowledging my presence in the room. She screamed at her breeder demanding immediate attention and accustomed to receiving affection was adamant to be held. Dianne had affectionately named this little girl Cricket.

*To anyone who has ever been owned by a cat,*
*it will come as no surprise that there are all sorts of things about*
*your cat you will never, as long as you live, forget. Not the least of*
*these is the first sight of him or her.*
**- Cleveland Amory**

When a breeder feels compelled to name a kitten it indicates a personable nature in that baby. Although many breeders will bond in varying degrees with their individual kittens, not many babies are provided with names. When you are visiting a cattery ask the breeder which kitten within the litter is her favourite. The breeder should not only express which of her kittens she finds the most irresistible but also the many reasons why the baby is so compelling. If she has named the kitten, chances are the baby has provided her with much enjoyment which will later be passed on to the new owner.

While Cricket sang a chorus to Dianne for attention, the only other available kitten was climbing my leg wanting to be held. I believe Dianne may have had a buyer for this sweet male because she gently reminded me that my sole intention was to purchase the female. True enough I had wanted a female but the Blue Point brother appeared more affectionate and was actually taking an interest in me. As though sensing my indecision Dianne invited me to tour her cattery. This was a welcomed change because I'd never witnessed a cattery in full operation before.

I was introduced to Cricket's father, who appeared content in his stud quarters, as well as two pregnant queens who were resting quietly in a comfortable maternity room. A larger rec room contained two litters of various ages. One litter playing on the floor were Blue Persians. I've always had an affection for the beauty of Blue Persians and was immediately drawn to a small female actively chasing her littermates. However as she was only five weeks old she would not be ready to leave her mother for several more months. Dianne once again reminded me that my purpose for being in the cattery and obviously taking her time was to buy the Seal Point female.

We returned upstairs to Cricket and her brother residing in the small bedroom. Cricket continued to ignore me and began chirping to Dianne demanding immediate attention. Although I considered Cricket's brother as more affectionate I agreed to buy the scruffy and loud female. After all she was a Seal Point, and several years had passed since I'd promised myself a Himalayan like the sweet little cat who had been lost in the storm.

*A cat has absolute emotional honesty: human beings, for one reason or another, may hide their feelings, but a cat does not.*
**- Ernest Hemingway**

In my purse I carried exactly $250 in cash. When I confirmed the price for the female I was told she was now also

$250. A couple of hours earlier while speaking to Dianne by telephone Cricket had only been $200. This situation occurred during a fearful period of uncertainty in my life when I was uncomfortable with any monetary confrontations. Therefore I kept my silence and never questioned the breeder as to why the kitten's price had suddenly and dramatically increased. Perhaps Dianne had a lapse of memory or possibly this was simply another situation with a breeder taking advantage of a buyer. I wanted the kitten and therefore quickly signed the Ownership Agreement and handed over the entire amount of my holiday paycheque. In preparing to leave, it occurred to me that in my haste I hadn't brought a carrier to transport my kitten safely home while driving. Cricket must have understood that her life had suddenly changed because when she was handed to me she silently accepted the inside of my coat as her personal carrier to her new home.

Cricket remained quiet as we travelled the 30 minutes back to my small rented home. Although we were strangers and she was experiencing her first trip in a car, she was comfortably settled within my coat. She appeared to enjoy her surroundings actively watching the road and passing scenery. As I drove, the consequences of my rash decision to immediately purchase this baby became sadly evident. I was totally unprepared for her arrival. At home there was no kitten food or cat litter and possibly I'd also disposed of my only litter box. Not having any supplies, I was left with little choice but to stop at a small convenience store about two minutes from my home. With so many rapid changes occurring I was well aware of how terrifying such an experience should be for a small kitten. However she appeared content to remain in my coat while we shopped for a limited supply of feline items to keep her satisfied for the night. Although I had a few moments of buyer's remorse, I was also aware that this was not typical behaviour for a kitten under such circumstances. Whom exactly had I purchased and would I live to regret my decision?

I entered the house carrying two bags of cat supplies with Cricket still warmly tucked within my coat. My mother's first response was, "Didn't you buy her?"

*The smallest feline is a masterpiece.*
**- Leonardo da Vinci**

I opened my coat to reveal my newly acquired Seal Point Himalayan female. Mark was napping and I was grateful the kitten would have some time to peacefully discover her new home. She appeared much smaller to me now that she was away from the younger litters in her cattery. She acknowledged my mother and then fearlessly set out to explore the extended space of both levels in our home. Half an hour later, Mark awoke and although I doubted this kitten had ever encountered a small child before she was equally fearless. She appeared more interested in my son than frightened. Mark was delighted with the newest addition to the family and squirmed in my arms anxious to touch her. However he could only watch her from a distance as he was still in diapers and needed to be changed prior to their physical meeting.

Caterina and
Jasmine's son
Mark

Many years later I still fondly recall this precious memory as a passage of time within my life. I was standing in Mark's bedroom changing his diaper with my mother beside me. The kitten was sitting on my foot looking up at the three of us.

"I think you should name her Caterina," was my mother's suggestion. For some reason, although I've always named my own pets the name was just perfect for her. "That's sounds fine Mom," I agreed.

My mother left within the hour and Mark and I had dinner while Caterina continued to explore our 900 square foot duplex. Several hours later Mark was finally ready for bed and I was soon to follow.

It is my belief that cats should be given free liberty when claiming their area of rest on their first night home. I went to bed and left Caterina exploring the living room. My bedroom was lit and I had the television set on low. I waited to see if the kitten's curiosity would also include seeking my company in the bedroom. After ten minutes of playing she must have sensed she was alone and started her familiar crying for attention. I waited in anticipation as now her breeder wasn't available and she only had me to comfort her.

"I'm here Caterina," I called. Within a few moments she trotted down the hall and came into my bedroom. She studied me for several moments before I lifted her onto the bed. The crying was immediately replaced by loud purrs. Caterina walked across my pillow and then curled herself around my neck to sleep for the night. I gently stroked her fur calling her by name. This priceless moment now frozen in time will forever be locked in my heart. For several minutes I cried silent tears of gratitude that she had been placed in my life. Whether it was the lack of love and affection within my marriage or the stress of caring for my beloved son simply didn't matter. In that moment we bonded and I loved her with all my heart. Caterina came to me during the most difficult years of my life and I have always considered her to be a personal blessing. The depth of my affection and my life long attachment to her has only deepened as the years have passed. To be blessed with a cat possessing such unique qualities can only be compared to falling in love with the right man. It only happens but once in a lifetime.

*There are two means of refuge from the miseries of life:*
*music and cats.*
**- Albert Schweitzer**

Mark, age 4, holding Caterina

# Conclusion

After months, sometimes years of working on a book, a writer searches for a conclusion to summarize countless hours of time and research. This was my situation yesterday with limited time to work as I had a dental appointment in the afternoon. Nothing is worse than facing a blank screen with a severe case of writer's block. There is also an awareness of the other contributing writers patiently waiting to hold the finished book in their hands. I simply couldn't find the correct sentiment to adequately describe the journey of writing such a personal book that was so near completion.

The contributing authors have been wonderful in maintaining contact and keeping me aware of any recent events occurring within their lives. During the editing process I contacted Sam, who resides with his five felines also known as *The Garden Ferals.* When last writing Sam had spelt White Paws' name with a lowercase 'p'. In writing his story I'd used a capital 'P' and wanted his e-mail included with the story to be accurate. White Paws is the beautiful tuxedo male resting beneath his tree as pictured on the book's cover. When I posed the question to him he responded by saying, *"I had not really given the spelling much thought, but on reflection it would probably be better with a capital 'P'. I'm sure if we asked him he would prefer it as it adds a bit of authority to his character."* Any correspondence from Sam is always delightful as he's such a quick wit.

After many long months of searching, Pat Chalmers finally found her new cat, a beautiful boy she named Sammy who was also seeking a new home. What I have found most endearing is her excitement in the many discoveries of Sammy's unique personality. Apparently he is quite different and yet as loving and affectionate as her beloved Barney. She had indicated that over the years Barney really enjoyed his food, especially her cooking. Sammy, on the other hand, is quite a dignified diner of his Mum's cuisine and leaves little evidence of leftovers on her floor. Pat wonders if Sammy will become a gardening moggie as well but only time will tell. Sammy is a beautiful two-year-old tabby who is so delighted with his new home that he never leaves her side, following his Mum from room to room. Although Pat will forever carry Barney within her heart, Sammy has also found his own place in her affections.

Pat Chalmers' new baby, Sammy

*Sometimes he sits at your feet looking into your face with an expression so gentle and caressing that the depth of his gaze startles you. Who can believe that there is no soul behind those luminous eyes?*
**- Theophile Gautier**

In writing the above I finally ran out of time and had to leave for my dental appointment. I've only recently met my new dentist, a delightful woman who somehow makes a dental experience feel more like an intimate gathering of friends. She's extremely professional but also very warm and compassionate.

After many years of fear and desperately needing dental work I finally sought counsel from my girlfriend who is a dental hygienist. Dana was aware of my phobia which had been triggered by an overdose of freezing many years ago. That experience left me with an overwhelming fear of all dentists which despite everything I'd tried still haunted me. Living with my phobia however brought forth a new perspective and empathy for others also suffering with my situation that I'd never truly appreciated before.

Due to my new dentist's care and the concern of her office staff my phobia appears to have dissipated. I'm so grateful to her for helping me to overcome my fear of dental appointments as they no longer keep me awake at night with worry.

I therefore entered her office only frustrated by an inability to fill a blank screen with a conclusion to this manuscript. My dentist inquired about my work knowing that this book was nearing completion. I confessed to being unable to focus and was presently at a standstill coping with writer's block. She smiled saying not to worry, that possibly an idea may occur to me while I was sitting in her chair. She mentioned that she always had her best ideas while jogging and not preoccupied by thoughts of work or other details.

Her dental assistant is kind and considerate, reflecting an aura of serenity that is common with all staff members working in this medical facility. I'm no longer internalizing the atmosphere of a dreaded dental office but one of pure compassion. I listened to the warmth of conversation between my dentist and her assistant and shared as best I could given my circumstances. The experience of being in such a caring

219

environment seemed to break through my writer's block. Before leaving the chair I was absolutely charmed by her dental assistant who was not only interested in this book but the others that will be following in this series.

"I like that you're aware that everyone has a personal story of importance," she said.

I thanked her and mentioned that additional volumes of true stories are planned such as *Every Mother Has A Story*, *Every Daughter Has A Story*, etc. I will also be accepting stories from professionals such as teachers, nurses and even dental assistants, for they too have a story to share. She loved the thought and said she'd enjoy contributing her story. My dentist also agreed as she had touched many lives during her career and had many touch hers as well.

Their excitement triggered an end to my blank canvas and I left my appointment anxious to return to my computer and write this conclusion. For truth be known, we all have special circumstances, people or pets that have contributed to and significantly touched our lives. For example, I had a teacher in Grade 12 who saved my life many years ago... and I believe his story also deserves to be told for I am forever in his debt. Although my love for cats will eternally remain close to my heart, there will be other non-pet books to follow in this series. I welcome stories from those not given an opportunity to honour an experience or a relationship that left a lasting impression and significantly touched their lives. Therefore the conclusion to *Every Cat Has A Story* is simply the beginning.

# About the Author

Jasmine Kinnear has been active in the world of cats for many years as a writer, Feline Behaviour Consultant, registered cat breeder and cattery mentor. Her distinctive ability to think just like a cat has permitted her to assist others in better understanding their felines' unique spiritual nature.

She is now embarking on a new path and requesting others to also share their stories to honour the special people and/or pets within their own lives. Her compassion, sensitivity and understanding of the human condition lends itself to the *Every Story* series of books.

Jasmine Kinnear presently lives with her husband and three cats on beautiful Vancouver Island.

Jasmine (left), age 5, with a friend and kittens while visiting her Uncle Jack and Aunt Frances' farm in Kirkland Lake, Ontario

Lightning Source UK Ltd.
Milton Keynes UK
UKOW042027140413

209209UK00001B/40/A